Encouraging Words

GARY ANDREWS

Encouraging Words

SPENDING TIME IN GOD'S WORD

Volume 2

ReadersMagnet, LLC

Encouraging Words: Spending Time In God's Word Volume 2

Published in the United States of America
ISBN Paperback: 978-1-955603-44-7
ISBN eBook: 978-1-955603-43-0

ReadersMagnet, LLC
10620 Treena Street, Suite 230 | San Diego, California, 92131 USA
1.619.354.2643 | www.readersmagnet.com

Cover design by Ericka Obando
Interior design by Renalie Malinao

Contents

A house divided cannot stand

Each time I have heard the President give his State of the Union address congress sits divided according to their political persuasion. I have never seen anything different until this year of 2011 when some of the congressmen decided to sit next to their opposing party friends.

This is a great step forward in healing the diversity that this nation seems to be going through. As most of you, I did not think much about the division because I thought that was the way it was supposed to be.

On June 16, 1858, Abraham Lincoln, upon his acceptance as the Republican Party candidate, gave his famous "A House Divided" speech to over 1,000 people. His long lasting and many times used quote was, "A house divided against itself cannot stand."

This was a paraphrase from what Jesus told the Pharisees in Matthew 12:25, "Every kingdom divided against itself will be ruined, and every city or household divided against itself will not stand."

Lincoln made his statement during a time of much controversy in the United States and was chastised by members of his own party for speaking this way. Why would any of us subject ourselves to criticism about this when our Lord and Savior spoke these words of truth?

Jesus went on to say, “If Satan drives out Satan, how then can his kingdom stand?”

I believe all of us as citizens of this great nation need to encourage our congressmen to work together for the good of the common man. Over the last 50 years we have allowed Satan to crawl into our government systems and take away many of our Christian inheritances and rights. It seems that in today’s society everyone has to be politically correct and stand for something whether it is what the Bible teaches or not.

We need to go back to the roots and beliefs that made our country the strongest and best in the world. Hopefully with this last State of the Union address and members crossed party lines to sit with their friends, this will be a good start.

Prayer: Father, thank you for a blessed nation. Thank you for the freedoms that you, and only you, allow us to have. I pray that the entire world will see our country as a Godly country and come to know you on a personal basis. Amen.

(Suggested daily Bible readings: Sunday - Matthew 12:22-36; Monday - Psalm 55:9-11; Tuesday - Luke 12:49-53; Wednesday - Galatians 4:8-20; Thursday - Jude 17-19; Friday -John 7:12-43; Saturday -Ezekiel 13:20-23.) A127-11

Do you know your destiny?

All of us are children of God and each one of us possesses unique qualities and talents.

What we do in this world touches someone, somehow, somewhere. We never know our true outreach to others.

All of us have dreams and visions of what we can accomplish and many of us have set goals on how to reach these dreams. These goals need to include what God wants us to do. I firmly believe that He has given each of us a destiny and it is our responsibility to talk with Him and learn what this destiny is.

John 14:14 tells us, "You may ask me anything in my name, and I will do it."

It doesn't matter what vocation we are in because all of us are called by God to do His work. Whether we are husbands, wives, parents, children, pastors, deacons, or just church members we are to serve our risen Savior and live for Him.

So many of us get caught up in worldly ways that we tend to let our call from God sit in the back of our mind. God has given us special abilities and gifts to serve Him. We need to lead the way in everything that we do, whether it is in our work place, home, social settings, or some other place that we are frequently at or in.

All of us strive to reach that golden age of retirement. We work hard putting our hard earned money into retirement accounts, 401K's, etc. We strive to have and long for the good life after our workplace experience is over. There is absolutely nothing wrong with this and God gave us the ability to realize we need these retirements and savings for when we are older.

As we strive for those golden years we need to realize we may never see the first day of retirement. During our lifetime of working and promoting the Kingdom of God through whatever we do gives us the retirement that is out of this world. Colossians 3:23-24 commands us to, "Whatever you do, work at it with all your heart, as working for the Lord, not for men, since you know that you will receive an inheritance from the Lord as a reward. It is the Lord Christ you are serving."

It doesn't matter what vocation you are in you are touching someone in someway. Remember, Jesus began as a carpenter and touched the lives of millions.

What is your destiny and how are you going to handle it?

Prayer: Thank You Lord for the opportunity of serving you and being your disciple. Help me get the world behind me and be a leader for You while I am on this earth. Amen.

(Suggested daily Bible readings: Sunday - Philippians 4:13; Monday - 1 Chronicles 4:9-10; Tuesday - Matthew 11:28-30; Wednesday - Proverbs 23:4-5; Thursday - 1 Timothy 6:17-19; Friday - Deuteronomy 8:18; Saturday - Philippians 1:6) A071-09

Everyday is a gift – use it wisely!

I recently heard a story of an older gentleman that was moving to a room in a nursing home. His wife of 70 plus years had gone home to be with the Lord and he was of an age that he needed someone around him most of the time.

Upon checking into the home, the young employee started explaining how his room would be and the color of the curtains and about the future.

The wise older man told him, "It is already decided in my mind that I like my room."

The employee answered, "But sir, you haven't seen your room yet."

"Happiness is something I choose in advance," remarked the older gentleman. "Whether or not I like the room does not depend on the furniture, or on the decor, rather it depends on how I decide to see it."

When each one of us rises from sleeping in the morning we have a choice of whether we are going to be happy that day or not. The Lord blesses us each time that we can face another day. It is up to us how we choose to spend it.

The new resident at the nursing home told the young employee, "I can choose. I can spend my day in bed enumerating all the difficulties that I have with the parts of my body that no longer work very well or I can get up and give thanks to heaven for those parts that I still have in working order."

Today all of us are running here and there and accomplishing about one half of what needs to be done. We sometimes do not think ahead and plan and only look at what's important, or seems important, at the moment.

God gives us everyday. We do not do anything to earn it and there is no way we can ever say that we gained a new day for what we have done. This is one reason that we shouldn't ever put off doing something tomorrow that can be done today, such as visiting a long lost friend, calling your family members and telling them you love them, or maybe, even going to see someone that you may not be getting along with and clear up any differences.

There are some simple guidelines that will help all of us if we will adhere to them. 1. Free your heart from hate. 2. Free your mind from worry. 3. Live simple. 4. Give more. 5. Expect less.

Prayer: Father, you are so good to me and I praise You for everyday of life that You give me. Thank You for Your many blessings and for all the friends and family that You have allowed me to have. Amen.

Suggested daily Bible readings: Sunday - Matthew 5:43-45; Monday - Proverbs 20:22; Tuesday - Luke 6:35-38; Wednesday - 1 Peter 1:3-5; Thursday - Psalm 31:24; Friday - Mark 9:41; Saturday - Acts 20:35. A058-09

Complainers need to think about reality

We have become a society of complainers! So many times, we look around us and complain about things or items we do not have and not praise God for the things and items that we do have.

I have heard many people complain about their job; however, we should all stop and remember the unemployed, the disabled, and those who wish they had a job. On occasions I have heard, and I am guilty of this as well, that some of the food I eat doesn't taste good. All of us need to remember in these type situations about the people that have nothing at all to eat and would gladly eat what we are complaining about.

All of us need to remember that life is a gift from God. When we are out and talking with others, we need to remember not to say unkind words because there are some people that can't speak at all.

I am reminded of a story of a young blind girl that felt so sorry for herself that she hated everyone, except her boyfriend.

She told her boyfriend, "If I could only see the world, I would marry you."

One day, someone donated a pair of eyes to her. When the bandages came off, she could see the world, including her boyfriend.

He asked her again to marry him. Now that she could see him, she noticed that he was blind and the thought of looking at his closed eyelids the rest of her life; she turned him down.

He was devastated and went away in tears. Days later he wrote her a note saying: "Take good care of your eyes, my dear, for before they were yours, they were mine."

Our human brain often works this way when our status changes. Only a few remember what life was like before, and who was always by our side in the most painful situations.

A similar story happened in Genesis, chapter 40. Joseph was imprisoned with the Pharaoh's cupbearer and Joseph interpreted the dreams of this person. All Joseph asked for in return: Genesis 40:14 "But when all goes well with you, remember me and show me kindness; mention me to Pharaoh and get me out of this prison."

Genesis 40:23 states, "The chief cupbearer, however, did not remember Joseph; he forgot him."

All of us need to be grateful for what we have and quit wishing for what we don't have.

Prayer: Lord, thank you for another day of life. Guide me in all that I do and let others see You through all my actions. Amen.

(Suggested daily Bible readings: Sunday - Luke 7:36-50; Monday - Ruth 2:8-13; Tuesday - Psalm 106:1-46; Wednesday - Hebrews 13:5; Thursday - Proverbs 23: 17-18; Friday - 1 Timothy 6:6; Saturday - Nahum 1:7.) A076-09

Hearing what our Forefathers said

The greatest generation is slowly becoming extinct and it is time for us "baby boomers" to pick up the torch and run.

As we talk and listen to our elders and the times of their childhood we need to pay attention because their wisdom will be irreplaceable. For many of us we have tired of some of the same old stories that we have heard over and over again, however after this time is over we long for those days of hearing these stories again and trying to remember what we were told.

From our forefathers to this passing generation we have been handed many excerpts of wisdom. Not only were we given tidbits of wisdom in each story but we were told about the dignity, discipline, and character each one learned as a child. Respect was taught in school and at home.

For some us we look back and see our parents as being hard workers with little time to share with their children. It may seem that they did not appreciate what we were doing and would very seldom tell us of their approval. It seems to me that we always remember what bad remarks we got and just gloated at the good remarks with out marking them down in our minds.

Wisdom comes through learning and experience. As this world changes and becomes more electronically oriented and gets away from the hands on type jobs, we are using our heads and minds in different ways that our forefathers did.

Dr. Eugene Swearingen once said, "The secret of success is to do the common things uncommonly well."

One of my favorite quotes I rely on is "the only difference between ordinary and extraordinary is that little extra."

The generations before us based much of their experiences and wisdom on hard labor and they accomplished it well. Today we are in a friendlier atmosphere of using our heads and getting work completed for us through electronic devices and other means. However this should never deter us from learning from our forefathers said and maintain their wisdom because it was them that brought us to this point in life.

In Philippians 2:3 we are told, "Don't be selfish... Be humble, thinking of others as better than yourself."

Our forefathers mastered this by learning that the most important words in life are: "Thank You." The most important word in life is: "We." The least important word is: "I."

Working together with and for each other will get our generation on the right track so that, maybe one day; we will also be remembered as a great generation.

Prayer: Father, thank you for another day of life and for your wisdom. I pray that I will learn from you through previous generations that you have sent before me and that I will hear them with attentive ears. Amen.

(Suggested daily Bible readings: Sunday - Psalm 111-10; Monday - 1 Corinthians 3:5-9; Tuesday - 1 John 5:18-21; Wednesday - Proverbs 8:32-36; Thursday - Matthew 12:42; Friday - Isaiah 40:13-14; Saturday - Philippians 1:9-11) A080-10

Neither money nor pride makes you rich

Over my many years of life I have seen many, many people who have accomplished many good things and gathered in the rewards that come with victory. Many have accepted these victories with humility and have given the opposition credit for trying and doing their best.

However, on a lot of occasions many of these victors have become prideful and boisterous on their claim to fame. They have put their comfort in front of their character, their popularity ahead of their principle, and become self-indulgent while losing their self-control. All of us can attest to the fact that we know many people that are of this nature and have also put their money and fame before and above God.

Jesus warns of this kind of person in Mark 8:36 when He says, "What good is it for a man to gain the whole world, yet forfeit his soul?"

Pride will do this to a person. Webster's New World College Dictionary defines pride as: an unduly high opinion of oneself; exaggerated self-esteem; conceit;

haughty behavior resulting from this; arrogance; sense of one's own dignity or worth.

All of us have a sense of pride and the world is continually telling us it is okay to be this way. What the world doesn't know is Jesus and His teachings.

Jesus tells us again in the gospel of Mark 9:35, "If anyone wants to be first, he must be the very last, and the servant of all."

So many of us get wrapped up in what we want or want to accomplish that we allow ourselves to be controlled by worldly desires and influences.

Charles B. Rouss once said, "Not in time, place, or circumstances, but in the person lies success."

We can all be successful and continue to have a humble attitude. All of us should be prideful in what we do, not for our glory but to the glory of our Lord and Savior Jesus Christ. It is okay to do a job and have expectations of seeing that the job is done correctly and to the best of your ability. The problem with doing the job right is that many of us want to say, "Look what I did!" Pride will destroy us if we let it. Humility will gain us trust and good will from all who see what kind of work we do!

Prayer: Thank you Lord for the opportunity of working with others. Let me do what I can to the best of my ability and that you get the credit, not me. Thank you for the many talents you have given me and the opportunity to use these talents as you see fit. Amen.

Suggested daily Bible readings: Sunday - Proverbs 8:13; Monday - John 5:41-44; Tuesday - Proverbs 28:20-27; Wednesday - Isaiah 5:20-21; Thursday - Job 40:11-12; Friday - 2 Corinthians 10:12-18; Saturday - 1 Timothy 6:17-19. A062-09

How to Dance in the Rain

I received this story not long ago from my daughter-in-law and the message in it is so powerful that I want to share it with you. The story did not have a credit line however it sounds as though the author was a very compassionate nurse.

It talks about love, real love, the kind of love that God gives to all of us each day. God's mercy and His love is so abundant that sometimes we mistake it because we are so busy looking for a four-leaf clover. All we must do is accept it and share it with our family, friends, and fellow citizens.

The apostle Paul tells us in 1 Corinthians 13: 4-7 what love is. Love is patient, love is kind. It does not envy, it does not boast, it is not proud. It is not rude, it is not self-seeking, it is not easily angered, it keeps no record of wrongs. Love does not delight in evil but rejoices with the truth. It always protects, always trusts, always hopes, always perseveres.

As you read the following story keep in mind that most of us take the ones closest to us for granted and tend not to show them our love as we should. God gave us our loved ones and we should love them as much as we can and show them each day how much we appreciate them. Let's try not to be so self-centered and take our spouses and family members for granted. Let's share the good news of God's love with them so that all of us can enjoy the day.

It was a busy morning, about 8:30, when an elderly gentleman in his 80s arrived to have stitches removed from his thumb. He said he was in a hurry as he had an appointment at 9:00 am.

I took his vital signs and had him take a seat, knowing it would be over an hour before someone would to able to see him. I saw him looking at his watch and decided, since I was not busy with another patient, I would evaluate his wound.

On exam, it was well healed, so I talked to one of the doctors, got the needed supplies to remove his sutures and redress his wound.

While taking care of his wound, I asked him if he had another doctor's appointment this morning, as he was in such a hurry. The gentleman told me no, that he needed to go to the nursing home to eat breakfast with his wife.

I inquired as to her health. He told me that she had been there for a while and that she was a victim of Alzheimer's Disease. As we talked, I asked if she would be upset if he was a bit late. He replied that she no longer knew who he was, that she had not recognized him in five years now.

I was surprised, and asked him, 'And you still go every morning, even though she doesn't know who you are?'

He smiled as he patted my hand and said, 'She doesn't know me, but I still know who she is.'

I had to hold back tears as he left. I had goose bumps on my arm, and thought, 'That is the kind of love I want in my life.'

True love is neither physical, nor romantic. True love is an acceptance of all that is, has been, will be, and will not be.

The happiest people don't necessarily have the best of everything; they just make the best of everything they have.

Life isn't about how to survive the storm, but how to dance in the rain.

Prayer: Thank you Lord for your love. I pray that I can be more like you and treat everyone with love. Amen.

(Suggested daily Bible readings: Sunday - Luke 10:25-28; Monday - John 3:16-18; Tuesday - Deuteronomy 7:12-13; Wednesday - Romans 12:9-19; Thursday - 1 John 4:7-12; Friday - Proverbs 8:17-21; Saturday - Ephesians 6:24) A033-08

Resolutions start with a pure heart

At the beginning of each year most of us will make resolutions for something we will improve in, lose weight, be a better person, or many other things.

Over the past few years I don't remember anyone saying that they are going to read God's word more, lean on God for understanding, go to church more, etc.

You know what I mean. All of the resolutions we make are things to do with self gratification or materialistic outlooks. Yes, it is great to lose weight and bring your body back into shape. Yes, it is good to cut out bad habits and develop new attitudes to make you a better you. People notice these things about you, however are they going to notice that you are spending more quiet time alone with the Lord, studying your Bible more, going to church on a regular basis, or just having a Christian outlook on everything you try or do?

If we do resolve to do these things, are they going to leave us as time goes by like all resolutions usually do?

Most of us are creatures of habit and usually follow the crowd. When one lets down then it is okay for us to do the same thing, and this causes us to lose our ambition and before long we are struggling again with the same problems that we resolved would not affect us this year.

As you begin the New Year, take a long hard look into the mirror. Who and what do you see? Are you satisfied with the person you are looking at and don't see that any improvements can be made? I doubt it.

All of us have something that we need to change in our lifestyles, and the best place to start is in your interior body.

Look at your heart. Are you a person with a forgiving attitude, a person with a heart full of gratitude, love, and a desire to see good in all people? If not this is a good place to start with your resolutions.

Proverbs 17:22 states, "A cheerful heart is good medicine, but a crushed spirit dries up the bones."

Jesus is the way to a cheerful heart. By accepting Him as your Lord and Savior your attitude changes and your outlook on life also changes for the better. We quit trying to do or accomplish things on our own but look to Jesus to be our source and guide in any situation or anything we try to do. This is also true for yearly resolutions.

Prayer: Thank you Lord for guiding me and leading me in the direction you want me to go. Help me get out of the way and listen to what you are telling me. Amen.

(Suggested daily Bible readings: Sunday - Matthew 8:1-3; Monday - Romans 7:4-6; Tuesday - Revelation 2:18-26; Wednesday - Psalm 119-33-37; Thursday - Ezekiel 11:19; Friday - Matthew 15:18-20; Saturday - 1 Samuel 16:7.)A123-10

Controlling your tongue

The old saying, "Although the tongue weighs very little, few people are able to hold it," is something that all of us need to keep in mind.

So many times I have heard people say something derogatory about someone or about some situation and they had no clue what they were talking about. So many of us are prone to repeat what we hear without finding out if it is true or not.

Many people, industries, businesses, and communities are hurt because someone will not have a good experience with whom or what they encounter and tell everyone they know the bad part of the situation. When this happens it is only human nature for us to repeat what we hear without knowing the truth of the matter.

I once had a pastor who said someone told him about a man's wife having an affair. The pastor asked the person repeating the gossip, "Did you see this happen?"

Of course his answer was no, but he was repeating it on good authority.

The pastor told this person if you did not see it then don't repeat it. If he was repeating something that was totally untrue then he was ruining the reputation of the person he was talking about.

The same goes with any situation whether it is a business, a church, a school, etc. Unless you witness the problem firsthand, you are only repeating something someone else has told you. In this case it could have been a misunderstanding and the person speaking may not be totally up front with what they are saying.

James 3:5 says, "Likewise the tongue is a small part of the body, but it makes great boasts. Consider what a great forest is set on fire by a small spark."

When you are talking to others about someone or a certain situation, know for a fact that what you are saying is the absolute truth. So many people and places have been hurt because someone repeated inaccuracies about a certain situation.

Prayer: Heavenly Father, help me to understand and know the truth when I am talking with someone. I pray that what I say will never hurt anyone or their reputation. Amen.

(Suggested daily Bible readings: Sunday - Proverbs 4:20-27; Monday - 1 Timothy 3:8; Tuesday - 1 Peter 3:10; Wednesday - Jeremiah 9:7-9; Thursday - Luke 20:20-26; Friday - 1 Samuel 2:3; Saturday - James 3:1-6.) A098-10

Thanks to our military service people

Several times during the year we, as a people of the United States, stop and honor our military personnel, especially our veterans. These are some of the finest men and women to ever walk on the face of this earth and they are giving or have given a lot of their time protecting our country.

Even though we have factions of people trying their hardest to take Christ out of our military, I personally don't think it will ever happen. Most of these people trying to put God out of America probably have never worn the uniform of one of the branches of military service.

Having had the opportunity to serve and be with people from around the nation, I have seen first hand soldiers call on the Lord for protection and guidance in whatever comes in front of them. A soldier, especially in war time, never knows what hour shall be his or her last. Families left behind pray hard and continually for their loved ones who wear the uniform of the greatest and strongest nation on earth.

Through our military we have been granted freedoms many countries cannot enjoy. We have freedom of the press, freedom of religion, freedom of speech, and many more freedoms that others can only dream of. Talking with and worshipping God is something that our military has guaranteed us without the fear of punishment.

Look at the history of America and you will find that our forefathers depended on the leadership of God and his Word, the Holy Bible.

Why is it that today people do not believe in God and put aside anything they think may be religious? Why is it today, after years of proving that God is active in our country, do we try and hide Him from the future generations of this great nation?

God is real and alive and very much in control. Each of us has the opportunity of knowing Him personally if we just believe in Him and that He died for our sins.

We have great faith in our military to keep us safe during our lifetime on earth. This adventure on earth is short compared to the eternity that the Lord has promised us. Have faith in God and cling to His word for guidance and leadership in all that you do.

Prayer: Thank you Lord for each and everyday of life that you give me. Lord, I pray for our military men and women and ask that you protect them in all that they do. Amen.

(Suggested daily Bible readings: Sunday - 1 John 5:18-21; Monday - Deuteronomy 20:5-9; Tuesday - Revelation 6:7-8; Wednesday - Proverbs 2:1-15; Thursday - Ecclesiastes 2:24-26; Friday - Psalm 32:8-10; Saturday - 2 Corinthians 4:1-6.) A075-09

The seeds of today determine the beauty of tomorrow's flowers

Our greatest assets for the future are our today's youth. We, as adults, have the responsibility to nurture and train these youth in values, morals, integrity, responsibility, ethics and optimism.

There is a Chinese Proverb that goes like this; "All the flowers of all the tomorrows are the seeds of today."

I am a product of the sixties and the hippie movement. I saw first hand when the youth of the country starting rebelling against all authority and renouncing all they were ever taught.

If it feels good do it! That was the saying of the day and most of the sixties youth participated in it.

Probably some of the problems we are experiencing today are because of the training the youth of the sixties have given their own teenagers of today.

Times have changed. We as parents of today may have waited too late to realize that we don't have the answer to every problem and that just possibly our parents were smarter than we thought.

A lot of problems in society today are because of our low morals, unethical values, lack of discipline, and no desire for what the future holds. Maybe our parents didn't care enough to discipline us in the ways we needed it most.

Proverbs 13:24 tells us, "He who spares the rod hates his son, but he who loves him is careful to discipline him," has been just a saying and something that we have not adhered to.

Now that we are the parents and the adults trying to maintain a trouble free environment for our children, we wish that our younger years could have been more of listening and learning instead of rebelling and doing what felt good.

For me, I am an optimist. I don't feel it is too late to pave a good road for a bright future for the young people of America.

We need to bring our morals and ethics up to standard and then pass on to our children the idea of doing things right the first time. We need to act and talk positive. Let's be more energetic about the future and teach them the values of what life should be about.

More optimism and good positive feedback are what our youth need. They need to feel good about themselves and the road they are traveling on. They need to have sense of direction and a destination that will provide them a safe comfort zone when they have achieved it. Let's teach them the difference between right and wrong!

Even though we can't correct the mistakes we have made in our past, we can help someone younger than we are from making the same mistakes.

It is up to us as to what the future holds for America. The seeds that we are planting today determine how pretty and bright the flowers of tomorrow are going to be.

Prayer: Father I pray for our youth of today. I pray that you will give me wisdom to lead in the direction that you would have them to go. Amen.

(Suggested daily Bible readings: Sunday - Galatians 5:16-26; Monday - Psalm 143:10-11; Tuesday - 1 Corinthians 2:10-16; Wednesday - 2 Chronicles 9:23; Thursday - Jobe 32:4-9; Friday - Psalm 119:33-38; Saturday - Philippians1:9.) A097-10

Senior wisdom can solve problems of the young

It seems that each day I open my emails; someone has sent me a good story with a tremendous ending. Sharing these stories on occasion allows me to new insight to people and their plights and/or pleasures.

The other day I received a story about an older couple that continued to live on a farm outside the hustle and bustle of city life. Their children were grown and moved on to the faster pace living and really couldn't understand why their parents wouldn't want to do the same.

On a visit home one day, one of the children began reminiscing about his youth and walked around the farm with his parents. They spoke about the great gardens grown in the past and all of the animals they have had. The family had been in the horse business for many years but had slowed down quite a bit from showing and selling their horses.

One of the older horses was still among the younger horses in the barn and the son posed the question, "Why do you keep the older horse? She is not a productive animal anymore. Sell her or getting rid of her would give you some extra money that you probably need."

Without hesitation the older farmer looked up and said, "We keep her because of love. Nothing else but pure love."

That evening after the son had gone back to the city and the farmer and his wife had gone to bed, the farmer was awakened by the smell of smoke. He looked out the window to see that the barn was on fire.

He couldn't get inside the barn and his greatest fear was that he had lost all his horses to the fire. He told his wife there was nothing they could do but to praise God for He had blessed them over the years. He told her, "let's go to the big old tree on the hill and say our prayers there."

As the older couple, during the coldness of the night, trudged their way to the hill so they could talk with God under the tree where they had been many times before. As they were approaching the tree, they could see shadows on the hill next to the tree and when they arrived, they found the older horse had led the younger ones out of the barn when the fire started.

The older horse had been to the tree with the couple before and her innate wisdom allowed her to take the younger generation of horses to this same spot when trouble approached them.

Life is like a fire to some of our younger generation today, just as it was when all our older folks were young.

Sometimes we get into situations and don't know which way to turn and then, through the wisdom of an older generation, we see solutions that can ease our problems. Just about every solution will lead us back to the God that has guided so many generations across this earth.

In most every situation we will find our problems are when we leave God on the outside and try to fix them ourselves.

The most valuable resources and the Godliest people will rank among the senior citizens of today. Be smart, pay attention to them, and invoke on their wisdom plus their trust in the Lord.

Prayer: Thank you Lord for our senior adults and for the wisdom they possess of past times. Thanks to you they know that you are the one and only true God and they are not ashamed to tell people about your Saving Grace. Amen.

(Suggested daily Bible readings: Sunday - Job 32:1-9; Monday - Psalm 111:10; Tuesday - 2 Corinthians 2:1-10; Wednesday - Luke 12:8-12; Thursday - Proverbs 8:1-11; Friday - 1 Kings 3:5-15; Saturday - Galatians 2:6-10.)
A131-11

When is good enough, good enough?

For many years I have heard the expression "that is good enough."

How good is good enough?

Many times, my wife has told me the task I was doing that I had done it "good enough". My reply to her was that I don't want to do it good enough, I want to do it right!

So many times, in our lives and, especially, in our daily living we are accepting jobs and completion of projects as being good enough but not complete or exactly right.

Where is the line being drawn on when we decipher something as being good enough especially when it is not completed or right? Why has our acceptance level come down from the point of perfection to a worldly standard? Have we all gotten in such a hurry that time is dictating to us on what is right or good enough?

What do we not understand about the Ten Commandments? They are simple, straight forward, and to the point. God has told us and taught us through His Son Jesus Christ that the only way to have eternal life is through a sin-confessed relationship with Jesus. We sin,

He forgives if we ask Him and our heart becomes changed with the purity of Jesus' message. It is not we sin; He forgives us and we do not have a conversion experience within our heart. This is not good enough!

The first commandment tells us, "You shall have no other gods before me." How many of us really obey this commandment? Too many of us put worldly values and treasures ahead of God and then go to church on Sunday, saying that this is good enough. No, it's not!

"Remember the Sabbath Day, to keep it holy." What a far cry we are from this commandment. Look around you and then examine yourself, do we really obey this commandment? No, we don't!

One more commandment that has really gotten lopsided is, "Honor your father and your mother." For us to do this the family unit has to be intact. With so many unwed pregnancies in the world today, is it a wonder that this commandment has gone awry?

Good enough is never good enough! God tells us the truth and what we must do to reap the benefits of eternal life. Listen to His quiet still voice and you will be amazed at what He is telling you.

Prayer: Thank you Lord for another day of life. I pray that I will be in tune with you and not with the world. Guide me in the direction that I should go. Amen.

(Suggested daily Bible readings: Sunday - Exodus 20:1-17; Monday - James 2:1-13; Tuesday - Romans 3:9-20; Wednesday - Psalm 1:1-6; Thursday - Ecclesiastes 5:1-20; Friday - Matthew 16:13-19; Saturday - 1 Corinthians 13:1-13.) A133-11

Try more gentleness and kindness

Princess Diana once said, "Carry out a random act of kindness, with no expectation of reward, safe in the knowledge that one day someone might do the same for you."

There is so much truth in this. I have seen over my years of dealing with people that everyone has kindness in their heart; however it is characterized by the environment they are in or have been raised in. I have seen people of different backgrounds and walks of life issue kindness toward others that many have never thought would be possible. There are so many people that are touched by what we say or do, and many of us don't realize the magnitude of just how far our acts of gratitude, kindness and gentleness will be carried.

On the other hand, people have done things that have affected our outcome in life, and many times we do not realize it until it is pointed out to us.

I remember a story of a U.S. Navy jet pilot that was shot down in enemy territory while serving in Vietnam. After his jet was hit with enemy fire he parachuted to the ground only to be captured and spend the next six years in a Vietnamese prison.

Many years after his release, he was sitting in a restaurant one day when he was approached by a gentleman.

The man said, "You are Plumb aren't you?"

The ex-pilot replied, "I am, but how would you know that."

The man said you were shot down over Vietnam after you had taken off from the air craft carrier Kitty Hawk and you parachuted to safety only to be captured."

The pilot said, "You are correct, but how in the world would you know that."

The man said, "I packed your parachute!"

The pilot, whose name is Charles Plumb, stood up to shake the man's hand and tell him thank you for the good job he had done on the parachute, because it got him to the ground safely.

Plumb is now a motivational speaker and he tells this story at most of his conferences.

Not only does he tell about the man that packed his physical parachute, but he tells of the ones that packed his mental parachute, his emotional parachute and his spiritual parachute.

After meeting the man, Plumb couldn't sleep and wondered how many times he may have seen this former sailor and didn't speak or acknowledge him. After all he was a fighter pilot and the other man was just a sailor.

How many times in life do we face daily challenges that life gives us? How often do we miss what is really important by failing to say thank you, hello, please, or congratulate someone on something wonderful that has happened to them? How many times have we missed a chance to give a compliment or just do something nice for a person?

1 Corinthians 13:4 says, "Love is patient, love is kind. It does not envy, it does not boast, it is not proud."

Can we honestly say that we live this verse? If we showed more kindness toward our family, neighbors, friends and everyone that we meet, this world would be a better place.

Are we packing someone's mental, emotional, or spiritual parachute?

Prayer: Father I pray that I can be the kind of person that shows kindness to everyone. Help me to understand situations around me and not be judgmental toward others. Amen.

(Suggested daily Bible readings: Sunday - Jeremiah 9:23-24; Monday - 1 Corinthians 13:4-8a; Tuesday - Proverbs 11:16-19; Wednesday - Ephesians 4:29-32; Thursday - Colossians 3:12-14; Friday - Zechariah 7:9-10; Saturday - 1 John 3:16-20.) A138-11

Dealing with uncertainties

Uncertainty is one of the biggest problems facing Americans today. All of us experience uncertainty and have difficulties keeping up because we just don't know the outcome of a particular situation.

There is an old saying that goes like this: "If you fail to plan, then you plan to fail."

There is a lot of truth in this, however even with the best of plans and intentions, some things just don't work out. It is a good idea to have direction in your life and strive to attain the goals you have set forth. It is also okay if some of your dreams do not come to fruition.

Many of us question ourselves on how to approach certain situations. In most cases there are no proven methods on achieving unpredictable jobs.

When this happens to us we sometimes get down and out and allow our frustrations to take advantage of us. Having to wait until certain dates to realize a true outcome, whether it is a new born baby, a financial investment, a job interview, or many other type situations, can take a toll on one's health and emotional state.

There is only one certain thing in life and that is we are all going to die. There is no getting around it, and no one is above this fate.

For us Christians we look forward to an eternity with Jesus. This happens when you realize that Christ died for you and your sins and he has paid your debt to death. Our bodies may go to the grave but those who have Christ as their Lord and Savior will live forever in Paradise.

Life is short on this earth and all of us are going to face many, many uncertainties. The only guaranteed outcome that we can count on is leaving this earth and going to live with Jesus, if we know Him personally and this is only through His grace that we can receive salvation. For this to happen we have to believe.

Prayer: Father, thank you for your grace and your love. Thank you for your sacrifice on the cross that I may live with you forever in eternity. Amen.

(Suggested daily Bible readings: Sunday -Psalm 119:121-128; Monday - Matthew 13:11-23; Tuesday - Acts 20:22-24; Wednesday - James 1:16-18; Thursday - Proverbs 27:1; Friday - Hebrews 11:8-12; Saturday - Daniel 12:10.) A090-10

Listen to God when headed to the unknown

Have you ever stopped to think about how Abraham felt when the Lord directed him to leave his homeland, leave his people and his father's household and travel to another land unknown to him?

This story is found in Genesis, chapter 12:1-14.

I'm sure that Abraham had many uncertainties about this sudden change, but his trust and love for the Lord was more important than anything he had on earth.

In April of 2010 my wife and I traveled to Charleston, S.C. on a senior adult trip. Being the one in charge, I had planned this trip and the entire itinerary. We stopped in Douglasville, Ga. on our way home to have lunch. It seemed as though cell phones started ringing in unison with people from Yazoo City calling and checking on their loved ones.

A major F4 tornado had just ravaged Yazoo City and many people were worried about the ones on the bus with us. These calls were coming from people concerned about their loved ones who wanted to hear their voices to ensure that they were OK.

There was much concern. For me it was even a greater concern because I didn't know what I was bringing these lovely people back to. Would they have a place to stay that night? Would there homes and belongings still be there?

Many questions raced through my mind as we headed home, but we didn't move the bus from where we were without going to the Lord in prayer first. As we traveled toward home cell phone batteries began to run down and communication was limited to me and the other driver. We were the only ones who had plug-ins for our phones and our entire group was depending on us for news.

Just as Abraham traveled and didn't know what he was going into, he praised the Lord for leading him in His direction. This group of senior adults is very resilient people and they also praised the Lord for what they would have whenever we arrived at our hometown. Fortunately, very few of them had damage and the Lord blessed our trip with safety.

The lesson in all of this is that the Lord is leading us. All of us need to stop and listen to Him and seek His guidance in where He wants us to go instead of going in the direction we want to go. If we will get on our knees and talk to God then the message will come across loud and clear. We just have to get ourselves and our selfish interest out of the way. God loves all of us, and we are His children. Just as you lead and direct the lives of your children, God will not lead you into something that will hurt you or damage you.

Prayer: Father, thank you for your love and your guidance. I pray that I will listen to you each and everyday. Amen.

(Suggested daily Bible readings: Sunday - Proverbs 12:13-19; Monday - James 1:19-25; Tuesday - 1 Samuel 3:8-10; Wednesday -John 10:22-30 ; Thursday - Mark 9:7; Friday - Ecclesiastes 5:1-7; Saturday - Acts 3:22-23.) A121-10

Everyone who got where he is, started where he was!

Discouragement can be a real deterrent to many people. Many of us allow the slightest disparaging word or statement to take us backward in whatever it is we are trying to accomplish.

There is a statement that says: "Don't' be discouraged: everyone who got where he is, started where he was."

I am reminded about Job and the difficulties that he faced in his lifetime. Job was God's man and was greatly rewarded for his love and desire to do what the Lord wanted him to do. God was so pleased and confident in Job that He allowed Satan to test Job in many ways with the exception that Satan could not take Job's life.

Satan took away Job's wealth, his family, his health, and his possessions. It became so ugly that his wife and friends told Job to curse God and die, but Job would not and his trust in the Lord never wavered.

In the end Job was restored to his good life on earth because he was obedient to God and did not let anyone on earth influence him in ways that would undermine his desire to please and love for the Lord.

There are many on this earth today that will tell you that life is what you make it. In many ways they are correct, however it is not the life on this earth that we should be concerned about, it is about eternity we want to live with Jesus.

Where we are today will take us to where we are going to be tomorrow. If tomorrow never comes, where are we going to be?

Living a life that is guided by the Lord Jesus Christ will take us from where we are today to an eternal home free from any strife or worry. We will be at peace and live in harmony with all the believers that have gone before us and the ones that will come behind us.

Live today as if it were your last. Live it in a way that pleases the Lord and not the world and your rewards will be far greater than what you can accomplish by yourself.

Prayer: Father thank you for another day on this earth. I pray that whatever I do and say that it will glorify and praise You. Amen.

(Suggested daily Bible readings: Sunday - Job 8:1-7; Monday - Matthew 13:11-15; Tuesday - Proverbs 2:1-6; Wednesday - 1 Timothy 1:3-7; Thursday - Philippians 3:12-16; Friday - 1 Chronicles 22:11-13; Saturday - Daniel 12:10.)A112-10

Know where you are going; Know where you have been

I overheard someone say that, "to know where you are going you need to know where you have been."

I believe this is a true statement. It seems that many people don't know the direction their life is going because they have not taken a hard look at where their life has been. For any of us to recognize where it is, we want to be, we firmly have to have control of what we have done with our life so far.

If you look at your life and like the direction you have been and seem happy in the direction that you are headed then you are probably a person of satisfaction, dedication, determination, and outlook.

If you are a person that is unhappy and not proud of what has happened in the past, then you are looking for the magic of a better tomorrow. The first thing you must realize is that if you are not satisfied with what you have done with your life, then it's you and only you that can make the change.

It starts with inner peace. I believe it is a heart problem that some people will never overcome because they keep reaching for something without a proper attitude. Inner peace only comes when someone is happy with the direction their life is going and has been. For many of you this inner peace will never come because you are reaching for the worldly desires of need, power, and self gratification.

For those of us that know Jesus as our Lord and Savior, our lives have changed for the better. We are not caught up in keeping up with worldly desires or looking at earthly items for satisfaction. We know that our reward is in heaven and that comes when we go home to be with Jesus.

As we reflect on where our life has been, whether it be what we are proud of or not, Jesus has the final resting place for us. If we haven't been faithful to Him or if we have been deceitful and untruthful to ourselves and others, there is still hope for you today. It is never too late to get on your knees and ask Jesus to be Lord and Master of your life. This begins with you and it should begin now!

Prayer: Thank you Lord Jesus for allowing me to know you personally. I admit that I am a sinner and accept your redeeming grace. Amen.

(Suggested daily Bible readings: Sunday - Luke 24:36-37; Monday - Job 17:10-16; Tuesday - 1 Corinthians 1:3-9; Wednesday - Ecclesiastes 2:1-11; Thursday - Galatians 1:3-11; Friday - Psalm 37:16-17; Saturday - Philippians 4:11-13.) A126-11

A cheerful heart is much better than stress

In many job opportunities you will be asked what you want to be doing and where do you want to be in five years?

It is a logical question and a very good one. It is a good thing to plan for the future and have a bright outlook of what it might or might not be.

I remember on one of my jobs in the early 1980's I was asked to project what my revenues and expenses would be five years out from where we were. At that time, I was glad to oblige having no clue at what factual answers I could give. The only thing that I could answer with was my very best guesstimates.

Let's reverse this role for just a minute and ask ourselves a question such as this. In every disappointment or disaster that is happening to me at this moment, will it matter in five years?

When we are struggling with our relationships, jobs, and other meaningful items of today, what will tomorrow bring for us? Will we continue to have the stress that we have put on ourselves and the people around us? Stress is the number one problem that creates health issues in so many diseases, heart failures, etc.

The only time on earth that we are given is this one moment that is happening now. Only God's people are going to realize this and try to live this moment as if it were his last.

Proverbs 17:22 tells us, "A cheerful heart is good medicine, but a crushed spirit dries up the bones."

Many of us allow Satan to attack us through our anxieties, attitudes, desires, ambitions, and self-motivated strengths and we in turn put undue pressure on ourselves and those around us. Jesus tells us the He is the Truth, the Way, and the Life and when we accept Him as our personal Savior, and then nothing else matters. Sure, there are going to be many trials and temptations, but we have to rely on the strength of our risen Lord to see us through.

Always remember however good a situation is, it will change.

We should always work to the best of our abilities and obey the laws of land and companies we work for, but not to the point where we are miserable and stay stressed out. Accept Jesus as your personal Savior and let Him have control of your life. Your actions and outlooks will change for a brighter outlook.

Prayer: Father, thank you for you love and guidance. Thanks for the privilege of talking with you everyday and for your understanding what I need instead of what I want. Amen.

(Suggested daily Bible readings: Sunday - Isaiah 40:28-31; Monday - 1 Corinthians 1:4-9; Tuesday - Revelation 21:1-5; Wednesday - Philippians 4:4-7; Thursday - Psalm 66:1-20; Friday - Ephesians 3:14-21; Saturday - 1 Peter 5:5-11.) A132-11

Are you waking up dead every morning?

When I was young and, as most children do, my brothers and I had our times of not getting along and would get into verbal spats. I very distinctly remember my youngest brother coming up to me after one of these spats and saying, "How would you like to wake up dead in the morning?"

I didn't think much about it at the time but it was some years later that these words really sunk into my thinking, however not in the way he meant them.

Accepting Christ as my personal Savior at the age of 12 I have always known I can trust Him and look to Him for inspiration, wisdom, guidance, and comfort. Over 50 plus years Jesus has been the center of my life. He has blessed me with a great marriage, four tremendous children, and now grandchildren. Knowing Him has allowed me to have gainful employment even at the times I may have been unemployed.

The Lord has blessed me tremendously. Visiting and talking with friends, relatives, neighbors, etc. has given me insight to what the phrase "waking up dead every morning," really means.

There are so many of us that are spiritually dead and out of tune with our God, that we are literally walking this earth with no reality of eternal life. Many of us self-professed Christians are really dead to what Jesus tells us.

In John 14:6 Jesus tells us, "I am the way and the truth and the life. No one comes to the Father except through me."

Research has shown us that no idols or other gods has ever made the statement they are the truth yet so many people walking today's earth believe in these false gods.

We need to wake up and face reality. When you die and leave this world behind where will you spend eternal life? Will it be with our heavenly Father or will it be as a member of Hades? We have a choice and we don't have to wake up spiritually dead everyday. Call on the name of Jesus and accept Him as your personal Lord and Savior and your rewards will be great!

Prayer: Thank you Lord Jesus for allowing us to know you personally. I pray that all will come to understand that you are the way, truth, and life, and only through you can they spend eternity with you. Amen.

(Suggested daily Bible readings: Sunday - Hosea 14:1-9; Monday - John 9: 35-41; Tuesday - Romans 9:30-33; Wednesday - Psalm 146:3-4; Thursday - 2 Corinthians 5:1-5; Friday - 1 Thessalonians 5:1-5; Saturday - Ecclesiastes 3:9-14.) A130-11

Giving of yourself and your time

As I grow older, I reminisce about the days of my youth and the days of my children's youth.

These are fond memories on both parts because what I remember most are the times I spent with my mom and dad when I was young, and the days I spent with my children during their formative years.

These memories are about spending time together and not about material gifts given one way or another.

As I reach the golden years of my life and try to understand what my children will gain from me when I go and live with the Lord, I was awed by what my oldest daughter told me.

"Daddy, what you and momma leave us will not have near the impact of what you have already given us. You gave us your time, your love, and you taught us how to love in return."

These were some of the most precious words I have ever heard. Most parents wonder if they have raised their children in a manner pleasing to God.

Even on the days we spend with our children and it seemed to be a waste of time on our part, it may have been the best of times on their part and a remembrance that will always remain with them.

Many parents of today try to buy the love of their children and most of the time these turn into failed relationships. What children need and desire the most is the time and nurture that only parents can give. In today's world many households must have two incomes to survive and be part of society. This is what is dictated to us from the world.

The sad part of today's society is that all the extra money we make goes into something meaningless and, in most cases, something we can do without. Children need love, time with parents, and guidance from their mentors.

Always remember that you may be only one person in the world, but to one person, especially to a child, you may be the world.

Give of yourself and your time to your children and train them in the way of the Lord.

Prayer: Lord, thank you for the children you blessed me with and continue to guide them. I pray that I can be the father that you want me to be and that others can see Jesus through me. Amen.

(Suggested daily Bible readings: Sunday - Psalm 127:3-5; Monday - Proverbs 22:1-6; Tuesday - Mark 9:36-37; Wednesday - Ephesians 6:1-4; Thursday - 2 Timothy 1:5-7; Friday - 2 John 4-6; Saturday - Proverbs 13:24.)A122-10

The most precious thing you can give your children

Over the past few weeks my wife has been going through boxes and boxes of what we have saved from when our four children were in school. She has neatly divided and marked the contents for each one of our children. We have anything from sports memorabilia, newspaper clippings and photos, to report cards, journals they wrote, stuffed animals, etc.

I remember a story I read about an elderly father that was doing the same thing we are. He came across his son's journal and remembered the journal he kept also. He opened up his journal to a certain date and it read, "Went fishing with my son today. Terrible day, didn't catch a fish."

He opened his son's journal to the same date and read one of the most shocking things he had ever read. His son had written in his journal, "Went fishing with my dad today. One of the best days of my life."

It is unique that two people can look at the contents of a day, after spending time with each other, and see it totally different. One saw the day as a duty to fulfill and the other saw it as a time to spend with his dad. It is a sad day when we, as adults, look on the time we spend with our children and grandchildren as a duty to fulfill instead of viewing the great joy that they can provide for us and we can provide for them.

My wife and I made a promise to each other that when we were blessed with children that we would grow up with them. We would spend time with them and stay active in their lives.

The Lord has tremendously blessed us and our children. Three out of the four are married and have families of their own. The fourth is a high school counselor and associates with teenage children every day.

Spending time with our children has been most rewarding. They continue to come home, and we are invited to their homes. It is a sad day when parents are so involved with themselves, such as jobs, social life, etc., that they have little or no time for their own children. It's amazing how many nannies, daycares, and others are raising children for families.

Most young marriages require two jobs to make ends meet. This is because the younger generation is always trying to have more than they really need or can afford. My wife was a stay at home mom, and this was one of the best decisions we have ever made. She is a certified schoolteacher but stayed at home with our children until our youngest started school. She then went to work when they went to school and came home when they did.

It was a great day when our daughter announced that she would be staying home with her children. She quit teaching school when her first child was born.

Time is the most precious item we can ever offer our children. Cherish every moment that you have with them because, and you can truly believe me on this one, time waits for no one and tomorrow they will leave your nest empty.

As my wife had compiled the items for each of our children, she came across a school assignment that my son had written. The assignment was to tell about his best friend. When she showed it to me big old tears came into my eyes as I read, "Let me tell you about my dad, my best friend." Memories such as these can never be lost or replaced.

It's my wish that all parents could spend more time with their children. Even with all the gifts we offer them and big ticketed items we buy for them, nothing can replace the love or the time we can give them.

Prayer: Thank you Lord for the children you have blessed me with. Be with them each day and lead them on the path you would have them go. I pray that our parents of today will give more time to their children and raise them to know you and your saving grace. Amen.

(Suggested daily Bible reading: Sunday – Mark 10:13-16; Monday – 2 Samuel 7:1-17; Tuesday – Ecclesiastes 6:1-6; Wednesday – Matthew 18:1-6; Thursday – Ephesians 6:1-4; Friday – Titus 1:6; Saturday – 2 Chronicles 24:1-2.) A157-11

Is your glass half empty or is it half full?

My wife tells me I am too much of an optimist and she may be right, but I am a person that believes anything is possible until I am proven wrong. My favorite verse in the Bible is Philippians 4:13 and I believe it with all my heart and soul. It says, "I can do all things through Christ, which strengthened me."

Being in sales all my adult life I learned the value of looking at situations and problems with an attitude of it can be done or it can be solved. Early in my career I learned the technique of assumptive selling. I believed that everyone had bought what I was selling until they told me no and believe me, I have received many no's in my life. Even with the no's I continued to believe that someway, someday, I would be able to convince this client that I have a good product and would overcome their objections.

One of my favorite books in the Old Testament is Job. Here is God's man put to the test by Satan with

God's approval. With all that Satan does to Job and his family, despite all the criticism given to him by his wife and friends, Job's faith never wavered in his mighty God. In the Holman Christian Standard Bible in Job 9:25 we realize that Job seems to have some pessimism, but never does he give up. This verse reads, "My days fly by faster than a runner; they flee without seeing any good."

How many of us today think the same thing as Job was thinking concerning our problems of today? How many of us have the faith in our God, which is the same God as Job's, to see us through our tribulations and bring us to the point where He wants us to be. Many of us are self-centered, egotistical, or lack confidence in our Lord that He will see us through any situation that comes before us.

I recall hearing many of my friends and co-workers say they couldn't make a sale or do a certain project because they were afraid or lacked proper preparation for the task involved. They were seeing their glass as half empty because they thought all the positive features were gone from the situation. They were seeing the negative side and not trying to visualize the good side. Don't many of us in this modern day and time do the same thing? Aren't we always trying to see the bad before bringing out the good? Are we a people that are afraid of risks, which make us prone to failure?

Job was a very wealthy man with a tremendous family. God told Satan he could do anything he wanted with Job and his surroundings, but he could not take his life. Job was God's servant and even though he lost everything he had, he never looked at his glass being half empty because he knew who his Lord and Master was. Because of his rejection to denounce God before Satan, God restored Job to his good life. God will do the same for us if we will not turn our backs on Him.

Whether you think you glass is half empty or full doesn't really matter if God is in control of your life. However, looking at your glass being half full makes a day look much brighter!

Prayer: Almighty Father, thank you for your love and your mercy. I know that anything I have or will ever have comes from you. I give you praise for my life and pray that you will lead me in the direction that you want me to go. Amen.

(Suggested daily Bible readings: Sunday – Genesis 31:17-29; Monday – Romans 4:16-25; Tuesday – Malachi 4:1-6; Wednesday – Ecclesiastes 4:1-3; Thursday – 1 Timothy 6:3-10; Friday – Hebrews 11:11-12; Saturday – Amos 5:18-27.) A164-11

When you can't find God, He will find you!

I remember a story of a young atheist who took a theology of faith course in a northern university. This young man was looking for God and on the last day of class he asked his professor if he will ever find him. The professor answered, "No, but I am absolutely certain He will find you."

The young man went on about his life and quit searching for God. At the age of 24 he was diagnosed with terminal cancer which changed his mode of thinking. He revisited his college professor and told him that God had found him.

The young man decided he really didn't care anything about God and decided that he would do something productive with his life. He told his professor that it is an essential sadness to go through life without loving. He also realized that it would be equally sad if he left this world without telling those he loved that he loved them.

How many of us today have this same story? How trivial it is for us to hold a grudge against family members, friends, or others we don't even know without talking with these people. Most of the time the differences we have are going to be very insignificant and over some petty misspoken words or deeds.

The young man related to his professor that the professor's words to him were correct. He told him that even though he quit searching for God; God found him. He realized that the surest way of finding God is not to make Him a private possession, a problem solver, or an instant consolation in time of need, but rather by opening to love.

When we love we find a life that is more beautiful that eyes have ever seen, ears have ever heard, or the mind ever imagined. Our most precious possession that we can ever have, and it is a free gift, is the Saving Grace of Jesus Christ. All of us need to remember that God is love!

Along these same lines we need to understand that the most destructive habit we can have is to worry. Our greatest joy is giving; our greatest loss is self-respect and our most satisfying work is helping others. The greatest problem for us to overcome is fear and the worst thing to be without is hope. We need to realize that the deadliest weapon is the tongue, the most worthless possession is self-pity, and the most crippling disease is excuses.

Our greatest asset is faith and the most contagious spirit is enthusiasm. Our most beautiful attire is a smile, our most prized possession is integrity, and our most powerful channel of communication is prayer.

Just as God found the young man with a terrible cancer, the man changed his thoughts and lifestyle from one of no hope to one of love. Love is what makes the world go round and the quicker we realize this the more comfortable we will be with our own lifestyle.

Prayer: Father thank you for finding me and giving me eternal life when I leave this world. I know without uncertainty that you are the one and only true God. I praise you for this time on earth and pray that I can be a witness for you and your glory. Amen.

(Suggested daily Bible readings: Sunday – John 3:16; Monday – Song of Songs 8:6-7; Tuesday – 1 Corinthians 13:1-13; Wednesday – Revelation 3:14-22; Thursday – Psalm 136:1-26; Friday – Job 10:12; Saturday – 1 John 2:1-6.) A155-11

"Never let the fear of striking out get in your way"

It is my understanding that the above quote is from one of baseball's greatest players Babe Ruth. I remember reading a book about how Babe Ruth came from a home for boys and through his skill of playing baseball, his will, and determination made it to the professional level and became a legend of the game.

I was reminded of this quote recently when my wife and I were watching a movie called "A Cinderella Story." As most Cinderella stories are, it portrayed a young lady whose father passed away when she was young and left her to live with a stepmother and two step-sisters. Even though the young lady was the rightful heir to her father's estate, the stepmother takes control of the situation and treats her as a servant. The movie shows the young lady going through the struggles of life without real parents plus having to put up with the abuse of her stepmother guardian and evil step-sisters.

As the young lady reaches her high school teenage years and with the help of dedicated employees from her dad's original business, she uncovers a quote written on the wall of his diner before it was covered up by his conniving second wife. The quote is similar to Babe Ruth's quote only with an addition to the end: "Never let the fear of striking out keep you from playing the game."

This is a tremendous quote and whoever said it first should be commended for this great insight to life. Many of us as we were growing up may not have had the confidence we needed to succeed without the guidance and tutelage of parents or a caring adult. The formative and teenage years can determine the direction of a life that can be a great leader, a scientist, a medical doctor, a great educator, a great preacher, pastor, etc. I realize the call to be a preacher or pastor comes from the Lord God however I feel that very select person needs to be around caring and loving adults.

In any profession we should experience the call from the Lord on what He wants us to do and seek that direction. The world tells us to be what we can and accept the results. Many of us that face difficulties during our lifetime will be sidetracked and go in a direction we don't like or want to achieve. This makes it very difficult for us to switch directions in our life because of the fear of change.

Just as the young Cinderella being told what she couldn't accomplish or do in life because of the evilness of a stepmother finally realized it was her life and she could make it what she wanted it to be. Many of us are told all through our lifetime what we can't do and never realize what we can do. The Lord tells us all through His Word that we can accomplish our goals if we trust in Him. In Matthew 7:7 He tells us, "Ask, and it will be given to you; seek, and you will find; knock, and it will be opened to you."

Just as Babe Ruth said, "Never let the fear of striking out get in your way," we should remember this. Life will give us many pitfalls and we are going to have our difficulties, however we shouldn't have a fear to reach out and accomplish our goals. When we fail at something we should learn from it and move on from it without reservation. Don't let the fear of anything hold you back because the Lord will see you through it, whether it is a failure or success!

Prayer: Lord I praise you for the life you have given me on this earth and thank you for all the successes and failures you have allowed me to have. Amen.

(Suggested daily Bible readings: Sunday – Matthew 7:7-12; Monday – 2 Samuel 7:1-17; Tuesday – 1 Thessalonians 1:2-10; Wednesday – Psalm 115:1-8; Thursday – Jude 20-25; Friday – Proverbs 16:1-9; Saturday – James 1:9-19.) A338-15

Saying one thing but doing another

As we travel this road of life we are going to run into all kind of people. Even though it is not our right to judge anyone, we, being humans, are going to label the ones we meet either through their actions, speech, mannerisms, the way they dress, or some other way.

Only the Lord God knows a man's heart and his eternal destination. People will fool you and whatever you believe them to be will on occasions be completely different from what you imagine. Some people that you think are very trustworthy will disappoint you and some of the people you think that can't be trusted will become your best friends as you learn their integrity and character.

I remember many years ago when I was driving for a charter Bus Company, another driver and I took a bus load of men to the Promise Keepers rally in Washington D.C. Among these great laymen of God was a preacher from a small community church outside the city where I lived. The trip was one that took 22 hours of driving and we only stopped to eat. We went straight to Washington

D.C., spent one night, and stayed a few hours for the rally, and then we came home.

The rally was phenomenal and the men were really pumped up and ready to get home to serve a risen Savior. When we were within a couple of hundred miles from home the preacher jumped up in the front of the bus and started speaking. He was asking everyone to share their experience and what the trip had meant to them. God had spoken to all of us and it became a mini-revival on the bus.

Even though this was a great experience for me it was also a disappointment as well. I learned that day that it doesn't matter who you are, the people that you think are some of the most Godly will fool you by their actions and their speech.

As the preacher was speaking one of the men in the bus spoke and said, "Let's go ahead and take care of our drivers," to which the preacher replied, "The drivers have been taken care of."

A week or so later one of the men came into my place of business and asked me if the amount of money, taken up by the men on the bus as a tip, was enough? I could only respond that neither driver received anything from anyone on the bus. He then told me they had taken up a good bit of money as a tip and asked the preacher to present it to the drivers. The preacher had kept the money for himself.

Some months later I read in the newspaper where this same preacher had been asked to leave his church because of him taking money that didn't belong to him. I am not sure whatever happened to this man, however I was very saddened to hear that a man of God was tempted and gave into the evils of the world. His desire for money and material things became more important that serving our Lord and Savior. I can only hope that he has been to his knees and asked for forgiveness from God for his sins and has straightened himself out.

There are many good people that have tremendous intentions and want to do what is right by everyone. These same people talk a good game however when it comes to walking the talk they are left behind because of their love for the world and worldly items. When we turn our lives over to Jesus we are to put away these worldly desires however Satan will always be at our door tempting us. This is why the Lord has given us the Holy Spirit to help us in our way and to lead us in the right direction.

Prayer: I love you Lord Jesus and want to thank you for loving me. Even though I go astray from your way at times, thank you for allowing me to confess my sins to you at any time day or night. Amen.

(Suggested daily Bible readings: Sunday – Romans 12:9-21; Monday – Jeremiah 5:1-5; Tuesday – Philippians 2:12-13; Wednesday – 2 Kings 18:1-8; Thursday – 1 Timothy 1:12-17; Friday – Micah 7:5-7; Saturday – 1 Peter 5:5-11.) A343-15

Trying to move forward without God

Contrary to popular beliefs, no one or no country can move forward or into the future without God. Yes, I know that many people have flourished and even some countries have grown to be powerful nations, however we need to look in the Bible at some of these same instances that happened in biblical times. The riches and arrogance of power are only for the short time and will not last.

One only needs to read the book of Genesis to see the rise and fall of many who became prideful and arrogant and how the Lord allowed their destruction. Adam and Eve lived in paradise with only one rule and that was not to eat from the tree of knowledge of good and evil. The Lord told them that should they eat of this tree then they will surely die. God then destroyed all life on earth with a flood because of the sins of humanity with the exception of Noah and his family and two of each species of animal life.

It seems like man would have learned his lesson after this and realized that the Lord is in control. As you read further into the chapter we see that mankind returned to a life of sin with more pride and even more arrogance and to this day it continues.

Just as the early inhabitants of the earth we have established our own gods and bow down and worship them. Our days have become filled with our own lustful communications and desires that we have very little or no time for the one and only true God. Even though we were once a great and powerful nation in America, we have elected subpar leaders and politicians who have given in to personal gain and wealth and allowed our nation to lose its prominence in the world.

The people of today are no different from those in biblical times. We have become so content with ourselves, our communities, and the people around us that we have neglected to fall down and worship God and thank Him for what we have. We have become a people who think we have accomplished everything on our own. We have become a nation that allows other gods to become more powerful than our God in our minds and actions. Yes, we are a prideful and arrogant people once again and our failure is before us.

Isaiah 66:2b tells us, "But on this one will I look: On him who is poor and of a contrite spirit, and who trembles at My Word." The Lord reminds us that our actions are unacceptable to Him. He created us for fellowship with Him and we as a proud and arrogant people have or are getting away from this.

Will you turn your life over to Jesus today and believe that His way is the only way. He is the only one that provides eternal life and it is free for the asking.

Prayer: Thank you Jesus for the opportunity of accepting you as my Lord and Savior. Help me Lord to rid myself of my pride and arrogance and to help others understand that you are the only way to have eternal life. Amen.

(Suggested daily Bible readings: Sunday – Isaiah 66:1-2; Monday – James 4:1-6; Tuesday – Psalm 59:5-13; Wednesday – Luke 10:17-20; Thursday – Jeremiah 48:29-30; Friday -2 Corinthians 10:2; Saturday – Zephaniah 3:8-12.) A372-15

If tomorrow never comes

Several years ago Country Singer Garth Brooks recorded a song called "If tomorrow never comes." When it first came out I really hadn't thought much about the lyrics but I did enjoy the music and the way he sung it. Many people are like me. They get so wrapped up in the tune and the sound that sometimes the lyrics just pass over our head.

"If tomorrow never comes will she know how much I loved her," is only one line in this beautifully written love song. The emotion that this song is presented with should be a wakeup call for all of us, especially if we are married, have children, or blessed to have other family members.

My wife and I have been married over four decades and are close to our fifth. From our first night together until today I hope that she understands and feels the love I have for her. We have four children and ten grandchildren and it is our hope that the love we have for them will be a reminder of what families are all about. Love for each other is the glue that holds families together and the family unit is what makes the world strong and a better place to live in.

Chapter 13 in 1 Corinthians is known as the "Love" chapter in the Bible. It is one of my favorites and love is explained in full detail what love is and what love is not. In John 3:16 we see the limitless boundaries of love that God has for us. In 1Timothy 1:5 it reads, "Now the purpose of this commandment is love from a pure heart, from a good conscience, and from sincere faith…"

For those of us that have accepted Jesus as our Lord and Savior pure love is more understandable even toward those that despise us. Worldly love is built on greed and lust and the ending effects can be devastating. I am not saying that anyone that doesn't know Jesus cannot love because they certainly can. They can have a true earthly love but when tomorrow comes and one of them is not there is that love going to continue? Many will say it can and I hope it does but do they have the hope of seeing their love one in eternity?

My wife and I tell each other "I love you" every day and through both of us having Jesus in our hearts, we will always be together throughout eternity. The same goes for our children, grandchildren, and other family members that know Christ and believe that the Bible is the inerrant Word of God.

A final verse in the song gives us an example of how we are going to feel if we do show our love to those around us. It reads, "'Cause I've lost loved ones in my life, who never knew how much I loved them, now I live with the regret, that my true feelings for them never were revealed; so I made a promise to myself, to say each day how much she means to me, and avoid that circumstance, where there's no second chance to tell her how I feel."

Live today with no regrets. Ask Jesus to be your Lord and Savior and understand the peace and love that only He can give. Tell your spouse, your children, your family, your friends, your neighbors, and anyone that you are close to about the love of Jesus for them and that you love them also.

Prayer: Father God thank you for my wife and the love we have for each other. I pray that when I am called home to be with you that she will understand the love I have for her and our family and that it will last a lifetime. Amen.

(Suggested daily Bible readings: Sunday – 1 Corinthians 13:1-13; Monday – Proverbs 10:12; Tuesday – Galatians 5:16-26; Wednesday – Psalm 63:1-11; Thursday – Ephesians 5:22-33; Friday – Job 10:12; Saturday – 1 John 4:17-19.) A381-16

To have friends, you need to be a friend

I think that each one of us should realize that we are special and unique. God made us this way He wants us to be this way and we need to accept this. In this world today we find many people, who want to change their bodies, alter their lifestyles, and go against the norm in everyday living. I believe that these type individuals are searching for something that will build them up and let them know they are accepted.

Something that everyone should realize is that God doesn't make mistakes! We alter His plans because we are driven by worldly values and go searching for better things than we have.

Many of us believe we have no friends and that the people around us don't like us and just tolerate our being. In some instances this is true but it isn't because of them, it is because of us.

When I was a youngster in junior high school I was very shy. I was afraid to speak up and state my case even when I had something to say. I kept quiet in class knowing that I had the correct answer to questions and would sit back in my desk waiting for someone else to speak up. My shyness led to some form of insecurity in the classroom because I was afraid to talk to my fellow students.

Yes, I had many friends but I wanted everyone to be my friend. I would search out the students that were shyer than I was and talk with them trying to help their ego. I would forego the opportunities of talking with the more popular students because I felt inferior.

As I have matured and gone in a different direction than most of my classmates I realized that if I wanted to succeed in this world I was going to stand up and speak up to make a difference. When one goes into the sales profession the first things he or she learns is that you cannot be shy on sales calls, you must know your product and speak to the advantages of it, and to listen to the customer.

I have learned through the years that even when I thought I was inferior to some of my classmates I was really their friend. Many that I have come across in my retirement years are very cordial and recall some of the good times we had in high school. I find that most of them are interested in where life has taken me and I am pleased to learn the direction they have gone also. I have overcome my shyness and the Lord has placed me in some tremendous locations allowing me to have friends throughout a vast area.

A friend from long ago once said that every time he saw me I was smiling. This is a trait that I have because God gave me happiness and I want to share it with others. There is an old saying, "A smile from you can bring happiness to anyone, even if they don't like you." This is a true statement and over my years of management and dealing with the public, I have found this to be a very worthy help mate.

The one friend that I have always had and count on is the Lord God. Proverbs 18:24 states, "A man who has friends must himself by friendly, but there is a friend who sticks closer than a brother."

We all need to realize that every night, someone thinks about us before they go to sleep. To someone else you may mean the world to them and this is why God made us special and unique. We need to live up to our potential and quit worrying about what others think about us and lead the life that God has allowed us to have. Be a friend to everyone whether you want to or not. It will pay dividends in your future.

Prayer: Lord I pray that I have befriended all of the people that you want me too. I pray that I can be the example that will lead someone to you. Amen.

(Suggested daily Bible readings: Sunday – Luke 5:17-26; Monday – Isaiah 41:8-10; Tuesday – John 15:11-17; Wednesday – Ecclesiastes 4:9-12; Thursday – 2 Timothy 1:13-18; Friday – Proverbs 17:17-18; Saturday – James 4:1-6.) A202-12

I want to live until I die

It wasn't long ago when a very wise lady told me she only prayed for two things for her life. She also told me she prayed for a lot of people and situations but she was only interested in a couple of things for herself.

She stated, "I pray every day that the Lord will let me live until I die." Many different reactions come when she tells people of this request. Many will furrow their brow and some will smile with misunderstanding written all over their face. However many people, especially in the older generation, understand exactly what she is saying.

I remember my paternal grandmother lying in a nursing home bed for five years before the Lord called her home. She did not know any of her family, had to be helped up and down to the bathroom, and on many occasions was fed through a tube. One often has to wonder the reasoning of the Lord when He allows a person such as this to live out her remaining years not knowing anyone around her or able to do anything for herself. I can only envision the Lord using this experience to help others gain patience and wisdom on caring for His people. My grandmother was a Christian lady and I remember staying with her when I was young and being carried, not sent, to church by her.

Many people today do not understand why someone would suffer and be a burden on someone until they die. These people may not know Jesus personally and doesn't understand His grace and mercy. These people also don't understand that when you accept Jesus as your Savior that your life on earth may end but your eternal life will be with Him in His heavenly home. Agnostics and atheists of today will tell you that the life you are living now is the only one you will ever have and that when you are buried you are through. Maybe this is why they are so burdened about the luxuries of the world and doesn't worry about anyone else but themselves.

My wise friend prays for these people often and hopes that they will soon find their way to the cross and understand why Jesus died for them also. She prays that they will find their way to the resurrection morning and understand that Jesus lives today and wants them to understand that His grace and mercy is free for the asking. One only has to go to Romans 3:23-24 in the Holy Bible, God's inerrant Word, to understand Jesus wants you to be one of His own.

My friend is a wonderful lady and a great, true friend. She loves people and she loves Jesus. She is about doing His work in everything she does. Her request of living until she dies is the same as mine. Both of us want to do God's work until He calls us home. We don't want to be a burden on anyone when we aren't able to do His work anymore and just want to be at home with Him.

Her second prayer is that she outlives her teeth. This also is a good prayer.

Prayer: Thank you Jesus for the life you have allowed me to have. I pray that you will take me home when you are through with me on earth. Amen.

(Suggested daily Bible readings: Sunday – Romans 3:23-24; Monday – Isaiah 28:10-15; Tuesday – 2 Peter 1:19-21; Wednesday – 1 Thessalonians 5:12-24; Thursday – Mark 7:5-13; Friday – Philippians 3:17-21; Saturday – 1 Thessalonians 1:8-10.) A212-12

Are you running from God?

Have you ever tried to run from God? Is there a certain place that you can go and hide from Him? If you have found such a place there are many Christians wanting to know where this place is.

Just as the minor prophet of the Old Testament, Jonah tried to escape the call of God by running away. God has called him to go and preach to the Ninevites or the Assyrians, people Jonah hated and wanted banished from the face of the earth. Jonah had no desire to witness to these people and thought he could run from what God was calling him to do.

There are many modern day Jonahs and each day becomes a hassle because of their unfaithfulness to the call God has given them. Just as Jonah rejected his call to go to Nineveh and got on a ship going to Tarshish, the opposite direction of Nineveh, many of us today are rejecting what God wants us to do. We have the same idea that Jonah had and think we can escape God's plans for us.

Jonah didn't want to witness or preach to people he hated. He didn't want to go and be around these despicable, treacherous people. He wanted to do what he wanted to do and on his own timetable. He had no love for the Ninevites at all.

Aren't we in the same situation in today's society? Aren't we called to be witnesses to those around us, even the people we disrespect or do not want to be around? Do we want to be associated with our enemies? Not only are we fighting these problems, but what about other circumstances we want to run from such as family, work, home life, and addictions?

Even though we try and hide from God there is no where you can go to escape Him. Remember He is the creator of the Heavens and Earth and there is not one place you can escape too without Him knowing where you are and what is in your heart.

God got Jonah's attention by allowing him to be swallowed by a big fish. Only then did Jonah cry out to the Lord and ask for forgiveness and tell the Lord he would do what the Lord wanted him to do. Many of us today are in similar situations however because of our pride, fear, and doubt we allow ourselves to be in God's wrath instead of His mercy.

God has a love for even the most unlovable people we can imagine and it is our responsibility to tell them the Good News.

Prayer: Father God, I give you praise for allowing me time on this earth. I pray that I will hear your voice and attend to any situation that you call me to. Amen.

(Suggested daily Bible readings: Sunday – Jonah 1:1-17; Monday – Matthew 21:18-22; Tuesday – Jeremiah 23:23-24; Wednesday –Ephesians 2:1-10; Thursday – Psalm 139:7-12; Friday – Acts 4:5-12; Saturday – Numbers 32:23.) A218-13

He never said "I told you so"

How many times over our lifetime have we told someone "I told you so?" If you are like me it probably has been more than you want to remember.

A lot of the time when we are in situations where we see something taking place and speak up about it saying that the result someone is looking for will never work. In the end the plan doesn't work, and we allow our egos to jump up and say "I told you so?"

We see so much going on in our world today that it seems to be a repeat of what the Israelites went through during their reign of wicked kings. Are we, as Christians, standing aside and watching the deterioration of our country and the world? Are the religions of the world putting God on the sideline and trying to appease the people by telling them what the world expects, and that God will bless them for it?

The prophet Jeremiah went through the same thing. He saw a world full of immorality, hypocrisy, and much idolatry. He was like some in our world today who stands aside and do not want to be involved.

God had other plans for Jeremiah just as He has for us. God had called Jeremiah the day he was conceived and had plans for him to fulfill the mission that He called him for.

Jeremiah knew that he was supposed to minister to Judah during the times of these wicked kings. He saw what God's people had become and stood back not wanting to get involved. He was so much like we are now.

Jeremiah was called the "weeping prophet," and for good reason. He knew what was going to happen to the people of Judah, but they did not want to listen. However, he did tell them where they were headed and what God was going to do to them, but the people were only interested in what the world was offering.

As Christians we know where our country is headed today. We are in the same situation that Jeremiah was, and we can only minister and speak to the people hoping they will listen. The Israelites would not listen to Jeremiah and was eventually taken captive and used as slaves by Babylon. I only wonder what God has in store for us.

If only we could get our people to read and heed to what Jeremiah 7:23 says, "Obey my voice, and I will be your God, and you shall be my people. And walk in all the ways that I have commanded you, that it may be well with you."

Even after the fall of Judah, Jeremiah could have said, "I told you so," but he did not. What about you? Are you telling people what God's plan is? Even if they are not listening and when God's plan comes to be, are going to say, "I told you so?"

Prayer: Father God, I pray that I can be a voice for you and that the people of today will listen to what you have to say. I pray for our country and pray that we will again turn to you for leadership and guidance. Amen.

(Suggested daily Bible readings: Sunday – Proverbs 5:1-2; Monday – Matthew 7:24-27; Tuesday – Deuteronomy 29:3-6; Wednesday – James 1:22-25; Thursday – 1 Samuel 3:11-14; Friday -2 Timothy 1:13-14; Saturday – Ezekiel 33:30-33.) A285-14

Keeping your head above water

As I was watching a program on television about what one should do in emergency situations, it occurred to me that as long as we are not followers and believers in Christ Jesus, we are always in an emergency situation.

The program showed a young mom and her son trying to go through some flood waters when their car became stuck and they couldn't move. As the rains continued to come down and the water started rising the car started drifting into deeper water and moving further from shore. The current was very strong and the son could not swim. As the car became more submerged neither of the passengers could get out of the car and it seemed as if their lives were soon to be over.

We have people all around us every day in this type of situation. Many of us are looking to the world for the safety and well-being of our health and bodies. There are so many people in this world that know the human body will die and life will cease as we know it on earth, but how many really understand that when we leave this earth that Jesus is waiting for us in a heavenly home?

Walking among us every day are people that have never heard of the saving grace of Jesus Christ. Many reject the message of Jesus and will never understand why Christians are not afraid to die. Many will live their lives without the knowledge and understanding of what Jesus will do for them and the promise of eternal life that only He can give.

The young mom and her son were very fortunate that a young man saw them in the water and came to their rescue. He was able to alert the fire department for assistance but without his help these two in the car would have drown. He risked his life swimming out to them. He fought the current of the rushing water and came to the aid of these two that were struggling to keep their head above the water that had gotten into the car.

We can also help those people around us by speaking up for Christ and telling those that we come into contact with about His saving grace. People are drowning every day in the sin of the world and don't understand that when life is over for them they have nothing to look forward to. Many non-Christian groups will tell you that when you leave this earth you are dead and nothing more will ever be for you or your soul. The Bible tells us a different story and we that read it understand that Jesus died for our sins and all we have to do is have faith in Him and believe in Him.

The young mom and her son lived because someone cared enough to go into the water and save them. They were able to live another day and speak of their salvation experience because someone cared enough to reach out to them and pull them into safety. What about you? Are you willing to listen to the message of Jesus if someone is willing to share it with you? Are you willing to read the Bible and hear the scriptures that will help you understand the saving grace of Jesus?

None of us have to leave this earth and have nowhere to go. Our bodies may die but our souls will live on in the bosom of Jesus and we will be with Him for eternity.

Prayer: Thank you Jesus for the opportunity of living on this earth and then going home to be with you. I pray that I may be an example to those around me and let you grace and love show through me. Amen.

(Suggested daily Bible readings: Sunday – Psalm 69:1-4; Monday – 2 Corinthians 6:1-10; Tuesday- Exodus 34:5-7; Wednesday – Romans 1:1-6; Thursday – Isaiah 5:18-21; Friday – John 1:14-18; Saturday – 1 Samuel 20:41-42.) A288-14

How do you forgive an enemy; a loved one?

Is forgiveness for an enemy any different that forgiving a loved one? Over my lifetime I have known many families that are torn apart because one or more of their members will not give an apology or let go of the past. I have seen brothers, sisters, cousins, and other family members hold on to grudges simply because of misunderstandings and/or treating one another wrong.

I wonder what we would do if God misunderstood us and took His time forgiving us for our shortcomings. All of us have them. There is never going to be a day when someone is not going to say something or do something that offends us. The least little thing can set off a time of hurt for someone simply because we are not forgiving people.

Most of us will harbor resentment instead of confronting the person who offended us. Many of us would rather talk with others about the problem instead of talking with the person we have the problem with. This only adds fuel to the fire when we talk about our problems to others and get them involved.

On many occasions when disagreements happen among family or friends, we call ourselves talking over the problem, except we are the ones doing all the talking and then cutting off the conversation. We need to understand that the healing process involves listening as well. Conversations should go both ways.

Many of us hold grudges against someone when they don't even know why we are being rude to them, staying away from them, or mistreating them. Many of us see problems when they really don't exist or they only exist in our minds. That is why talking to one another is so important.

Many years ago I had two young ladies that worked with me and during the day became agitated at each other. Their behavior not only affected our department but it spread out to the customers as well. At the end of the day I called the entire staff out of the building and confronted the young ladies about the problems. When the time came for them to accuse one another neither remembered why they were angry with each other, they just held on to their needless resentment. The situation resolved itself with proper communication.

Remember the story told to us in Genesis 45:4-15 when Joseph was sold by his brothers to a traveling caravan which sold him into slavery. Years later Joseph confronted his brothers in their time of need but he forgave them. How many of us in this day and time would even think about forgiving someone that had robbed us of years of not being with our family and loved ones.

Webster's Dictionary tells us that to forgive is to give up resentment against or the desire to punish; stop being angry with; pardon. The Bible tells us in Luke 17:3-4; "Take heed to yourselves. If your brother sins against you, rebuke him; and if he repents, forgive him. And if he sins against you seven times in a day, and seven times in a day returns to you, saying I repent, you shall forgive him."

Forgiveness begins with an open heart plus open communication with skills of listening. It also includes love on part of the offended and faith in the offender.

Jesus forgives us of all of our transgressions if we will go to Him and ask Him to. Most all of our problems of forgiveness could be handled through prayer and open communication with others. Why would any of us carry around a load of resentment and harbor hatred when there is no need to.

Prayer: Thank you God for hearing my prayers. Thank you for all of my brothers and sisters and I pray that if I have offended any of them that they will come to me and allow me to ask for forgiveness. Amen.

(Suggested daily Bible readings: Sunday – Romans 5:6-11; Monday – Genesis 50:15-21; Tuesday – Matthew 18:21-35; Wednesday – Psalm 25:8-11; Thursday – Hebrews 1:1-4; Friday – Jeremiah 50:20; Saturday – 1 Peter 4:7-11.) A259-13

Good work ethics come from guidance and leadership

Having the opportunity of watching my grandson play summer baseball has been something I have really enjoyed. To see his team, play and perform at the level they have accomplished is a reward of their dedication and hard work. Their game style work ethics during their practice sessions have prepared them to be one of the best little league teams I have ever seen.

They have been pushed by their coaches and parents to be better than their expectations. These young minds have accomplished this and their performance on and off the field are to be commended. The discipline required of them to be a part of this squad requires good morals, good work ethics, quick thinking, and common courtesy.

This has been good training for them as they approach their teen years and some of the most versatile times they will ever go through. They are going to become adults and if they will continue in this line of thinking they will become leaders of tomorrow.

So many times, we see people struggling in today's world and the reason is they have either forgotten their childhood upbringing or they had a poor childhood upbringing. In some cases, and this includes today's society, children must raise themselves due to lack of parental guidance and/or no leadership. But even in these scenarios these children will look to someone for their guidance whether it is a bad or good experience.

As our younger generation continues to grow up, we as adults need to continue to nurture them in the ways of our Lord. Let them see us with the high Christian morals we were taught, and they have learned as young children and allow them to grow up with people that care about them. We need to be responsible for our actions and not allow ourselves to forget who is watching and following us. Children of today are hungry for guidance and leadership. If we fail to do our jobs, then they are going to follow someone that will provide alternative methods. Let us not fail in our duties as grownups and parents. All of us need to show them Christian values in all that we do.

Prayer: Father God, thank you for the examples you have given to us. Let us take these examples and use them through our lives so that we can be living testaments for you. Amen.

(Suggested daily Bible readings: Sunday – Romans 13:1-7; Monday – 2 Timothy 3:16; Tuesday - Deuteronomy 18:18; Wednesday - 1 Timothy 4:12; Thursday – Psalm 119:105; Friday – Exodus 20:8; Saturday – Revelation 22:18.) A143-11

Being a person of integrity and good character

Many years ago, when I was fresh out of the Air Force and finishing my last year of college, I worked for Sears and Roebuck in sales.

I met and dealt with a lot of people. Many of my co-workers became close friends and we built a trust in our relationships.

For some reason I was having a difficult time one day, dealing with a customer. It was a situation I couldn't win because whatever I said I was wrong. The customer became obnoxious and belligerent and asked to talk with my manager.

I am not sure the manager ever satisfied this person and I'm not sure anyone could have at that time. Anyway, after the situation was over, I approached my manager and asked why the customer was so angry.

I will never forget his reply and his words have stuck with me for the last 30-plus years.

He said, "The problem is that this customer will never be satisfied with anything. The difference between you and him is that you are a person of integrity."

Integrity! What is the definition of integrity?

I knew what it was, but I wanted to read Webster's definition of it just to be sure we were on the same page. A portion of Webster's definition states, "the quality or state of being of sound moral principle; uprightness, honesty, and sincerity."

What a compliment! My manager told me it defined my character.

I have never forgotten his words and will always be appreciative of what he told me. I have tried to pattern my thinking after his and uplift and encourage the people around me and that I work with. Character is having a moral constitution, moral strength, self-discipline, fortitude, along with a good reputation. It speaks of good behavior and qualities.

It is my hope and prayer that everyone can be a person of integrity and good character. I firmly believe that if we would study God's Word, we could become the person that God wants us to be and all of us would be better servants for His kingdom. Remember what the apostle Paul said in Philippians 4:8; "Finally, brothers, whatever is true, whatever is noble, whatever is right, whatever is pure, whatever is lovely, whatever is admirable, if anything is excellent or praiseworthy, think about such things."

Prayer: Lord I ask that You lead me in the direction that I can serve you and only you. Give me strength to be a person of integrity and Godly character. Amen.

(Suggested daily Bible readings: Sunday – 1 John 4:7-11; Monday - Proverbs 20:23-29; Tuesday - Matthew 6:16-18; Wednesday – Psalm 15:1-5; Thursday - Luke 8:11-15; Friday - Numbers 23:19; Saturday – Mark 9:42-50.) A093-10

Is your life running on empty?

Several years ago, I drove a chartered bus to Ft. Worth, TX, with a group of senior adults on board. They were going to a senior adult conference held in downtown Ft. Worth. Even though this was only a part time job for me I was considered lead driver and one that took good care of the bus and its passengers.

This particular trip I had everything in order and insured that these senior adults got to where they were going. I drove from Mississippi to Texas, ran around Ft. Worth to several locations and made several trips from the motel to the convention center. I had been a driver for several years and considered myself to be ahead of the game when it came to have plenty of fuel in the bus. This time I miscalculated and in the middle of town around 9 p.m. I exited the convention center only to go about 100 feet. There I sat in the middle of the road with a bus load of tired senior citizens.

I learned a valuable lesson from this experience. Even though I thought I had everything planned out, I allowed the bus to run out of fuel.

Many times, during our lifetime we think we have our lives in order only to find out we are not where we should be. In our workplace, in our social life, in our church activities, with our family and friends, we seem to be okay on the outside when we are running on fumes and need to be recharged. Many times, this will happen when we isolate ourselves from others and not feed off of their energy.

This is especially true when we quit attending church. So many of us tend to think we can sit at home, go fishing, or attend other functions we deem more important than fellowship with Christians. I have heard many people say that I don't need the church. I can worship on my own terms by praying and reading the Bible.

This is not untrue but being alone and studying your Bible will give you a self-satisfaction that will not be shared with others. Look at what the apostle Paul said in Romans 15:14; "I myself am convinced, my brothers, that you yourselves are full of goodness, complete in knowledge and competent to instruct one another."

Not going to church or sharing your faith with others will eventually leave you feeling empty on the inside. We need to do as Jesus taught us through the Great Commission in Matthew 28:18-20. Verse 19 states "Go ye therefore, and teach all nations, baptizing them in the name of the Father, and of the Son, and of the Holy Ghost."

Just as I allowed the bus I was driving to run out of fuel, which took 14 hours to correct and get on the road again, our lives can also run out of gas. I should have taken a closer look and better care of what I was doing, and I wouldn't have let the people down that were with me. Incidentally, all of the senior adults were shuttled to their hotel by another bus and did not sit in the bus all night.

Are you running on empty? Only you can tell.

Prayer: Father, again I thank you for another day of life. Thank you for your many blessings and I ask that you continue to bless me in everything that I do. Let me serve you with a full tank of gas and not run empty. Amen.

(Suggested daily Bible readings: Sunday – Job 14:1-6; Monday – Matthew 28:16-20; Tuesday – Amos 3:3; Wednesday – James 4:7-11; Thursday –Micah 6:9-16; Friday – Acts 2:42-47; Saturday – Proverbs 15:29-33.)
A144-11

Are you on a one-way street going the wrong direction?

Have you ever driven your car down a street and realized it was a one-way street and you were going the wrong way? Several years ago, I drove a group of high school children to New Orleans and got on a one-way street going the wrong way.

During this little adventure in New Orleans, and me not being familiar with the streets, found myself on some back streets that were poorly lit and not well signed. I had no idea I was going the wrong way and neither did the chaperones or students until we passed a one-way sign with the arrow pointing the other way.

Many of us in our daily routines of work and social life may not realize the direction that we are heading. Even though it may seem as if all is well in our life, we could be headed for a downfall and have no one there with us to lift us up. And, from another perspective, we may have people around us that are headed for destruction and we are not leading or helping them find the righteous track.

Doris Mortman once stated, "Unless you make peace with who you are, you will never be content with what you have." The problem with many of us today is that we believe we are happy with the material possessions we have and would be much happier with things we do not have. With this in mind we push ourselves and the people around to achieve material possessions and not worry about their spiritual well-being or ours.

Many times, we are so wrapped up about what we can own or have and never realize we are on a one-way street headed the wrong way. For us to stay focused on what is important we must discipline ourselves. We must understand what we accumulate on earth means nothing, however if we miss out on eternal life, we have lost everything.

Please understand that I am for doing the best you can while you are on this earth but do it the best you can through the guidance of the Holy Spirit and be Spirit filled in all that you say or do.

Proverbs 12:3 tells us, "A man cannot be established through wickedness, but the righteous cannot be uprooted."

The Saving Grace of Jesus Christ is all that we will ever need while we walk these meaningless days on earth. If you do well while on earth and it's through the grace of God, use your abundance and wealth for the kingdom of

God. It is easy for us to get on a one-way street going the wrong way but realizing where we are headed with our life and what our destination is, will get us turned around and headed in the right direction.

Prayer: Lord lead me in the direction you want me to go. Help me get out of your way and allow you to touch others through my life. Amen.

(Suggested daily Bible readings: Sunday -1 Corinthians 9:24-27; Monday – Luke 3:7-17; Tuesday – Psalm 18:20-24; Wednesday – Philippians 3:12-16; Thursday – Deuteronomy 20:5-9; Friday – Leviticus 20:26; Saturday – Romans 16:17-20.) A153-11

Building bridges that last forever

On our way home from a camping trip we were crossing a lake in the North Georgia mountains. It is a beautiful lake with scenic views that are tremendous and only God can create. As we boarded the bridge, which was very long, I wondered how many years ago it was built. It was an old structure with steel beams running along the side of us, below us, and over us.

Our trust in this faithful old bridge was true to the level that we trusted it completely. It was built by men and women we will never meet because most of them live with the Lord, hopefully all the ones that have gone on before us do! This bridge is probably between 80 to 100 years old, but the structure was sound and people trusted it to get them to the other side.

This bridge reminded me of a poem I have read many times. It is called the "Builder" and I wish I knew the author, but I do not. It is about life and what I am doing to contribute to it. Everyone should read this poem and look within themselves to see if they are a wrecker of life or a builder to those around us.

Each day our faith in God is tested and the way we react to these tests are seen by those who follow us. Our children, brothers, sisters, spouses, friends, neighbors, and even people we do not know are watching us. How we handle adversity and problems of life will forever be etched in someone's mind whether we realize it or not. The Bible tells us in Proverbs 22:6, "Train up a child in a way he should go; even when he is old he will not depart from it."

I am printing the words of the poem I mentioned hoping that it will have the same meaning to you as it has with me.

A Poem by an Unknown Author:
"The Builder"

I saw a group of men in my hometown; A
group of men tearing a building down

With a heave and a ho and mighty yell;
They swung a beam and an entire wall fell

I asked the supervisor, "Are these men
skilled? The type you'd hire if you wanted
to build?"

And he laughed and said, "Why no indeed!
Common labor, people with no talent is
all I need

For I can tear down in a day or two; What
it took a builder years to do"

And I thought to myself as I walked away;
Which of the roles am I going to play?

Am I one who is tearing down; As I
carelessly make my way around?

Or am I one who builds with care; In hopes
that my friends

(my brothers and sisters) will be glad I was
there?

The bridge that we were crossing over the lake on has stood the test of time because of the skilled labor that built it. We are grateful that it has, and it got us over the lake with no problems because someone cared to do it right and help those that were coming behind them. Our lives are much like this bridge. Are we looking to God to carry us through this life on earth and are we building a bridge for those who are following us? Will our bridge stand the test of time for everyone to say, "Thank you for thinking of me as you went through life and sowing the seeds of righteousness, hard work, a great attitude, and a love for God who sees and knows everything? Each one of us has the option of being a wrecker or a builder. Which one will you choose?

Prayer: Thank you Lord Jesus for the opportunity that you have given me on earth. I pray that I can be the one to strengthen others and build a bridge for them to cross over as they go through life. Amen

(Suggested daily Bible readings: Sunday – 2 Peter 1:1-15; Monday – Malachi 3:8-12; Tuesday – Romans 12:9-21; Wednesday – Psalm 40:6-10; Thursday – Ephesians 4:25-32; Friday – Isaiah 40:6-8; Saturday – Galatians 5:16-26.) A435-17

Where have all the flowers gone?

In the early 60's there was a very popular folk song called, "Where have all the flowers gone?" written by Pete Seeger. This song has been recorded by many artists and in many languages.

Considered to be a political song the message is very strong and has so much meaning. Many say it talks about the struggles of anger and war among the nations, but some have said it speaks also to the inner struggles of man with himself. The phrase "When will they ever learn," is the endless battle within all of us and passes from generation to generation.

I think about this song in a different but similar way. I firmly believe that all of us could sing this song and not talk about the warfare within us but to the wisdom that has escaped us through the loss of older and wiser generations. Seeger's song relates to young girls plucking the flowers and then the young girls being picked by the young men for their wives. The men go off to war and return to graveyards, which again produces flowers for the young girls to go and pluck again. It is a rotation that seems to never cease.

Thinking back to when I was a teenager, I wish that I had spent more time listening and learning from the previous generation. Even though we are in the midst of the most advanced electronic age, have we learned the basics of life or are we just getting by with imitations that will soon fade into obscurity? What has happened to common courtesy? Where has the respect of elders gone to? What about the reverence of Sunday and God's house?

We have become a generation of fast food, less family time, impatience, rudeness, little or no hospitality, self-centeredness, laziness, and, for many, Godlessness. The world moves in a fast-circular motion and people are continuing to look about and wonder why we are changing to the immoral and unethical values that are so prevalent today. Why have we quit standing up and speaking up for God? Why are we allowing radical religions to dictate to us what we should or should not be doing? Little by little Satan and his force of demons are taking away our freedoms that our previous generations treasured and stood up for.

Where have all the flowers gone? Gone to graveyards everyone, when will we ever learn? If we continue this path of destruction and our non-obedience to the one and only true God, then we will go to graveyards with no legacy to leave to our future generations. The future starts now and if we are not willing to stand and fight for what we know is right, then we have no hope. We need to hear and heed the psalmist words in Psalm 37:1-2: "Do not fret because of evil men or be envious of those who do wrong; for like the grass they will soon wither, like green plants they will soon die away."

Prayer: Father thank you for another day of life. I pray that the life I lead will be a testament to the ones that follow me. I pray for our sinful world and pray that our country will return to you. Amen.

(Suggested daily Bible readings: Sunday – Psalm 73:2-28; Monday – Luke 10:18-23; Tuesday – Proverbs 24:19-22; Wednesday – 1 Corinthians 11:17-22; Thursday - Job 17:1-16; Friday – 1 Peter 2:23; Saturday – Exodus 10:1-2.) A159-11

Leaving this world with regrets

Have you ever heard anyone say that I have lived my life the way I wanted and have absolutely no regrets? If you have this must have been a very contented person and left no stone unturned. Most of the time when someone is on their death bed you will hear them say I wish I had taken more time to do… or I wish I had done so and so.

Life is short and many people have desires to do certain things, but they are always putting them off until tomorrow. For many, tomorrow never comes and they leave this earth with unfilled dreams.

When my wife and I first married I was in the Air Force and stationed in Colorado Springs, CO. We had aspirations of snow skiing since neither of us had ever tried it before. Being in Colorado over the winter, ample opportunities came and went for us to ski however we kept putting it off and eventually we moved back to our home state. We did say that one day we would come back and visit this beautiful state again and snow ski but as fate would have it, we haven't done this yet. Our dream of nearly 50 years ago hasn't been fulfilled and now I am much older and way out of physical condition to try this sport.

My regret of not skiing doesn't even compare to those that have memories of something they are not proud of. My regret is not even close to someone who has or had problems with family, friends, or others and simply would not put aside their pride and go to these people to resolve the issues between them.

Many have unconfessed sin and are not willing to let go of worldly ways and confess these sins to God. For the ones of us that know Jesus as our Lord and Savior we are convicted by the Holy Spirit of these sins and all we must do is go to our knees and ask forgiveness from the Lord. For those that have problems with people around us for something said that hurt us or them, we need to go to these people and make things right. Even if we are on the receiving end of the hurt, shame, or disagreement we can be the bigger person and approach the one that hurt us to correct the issue.

The prince of the earth, Satan, is always lurking around and will do anything to keep us from being happy in the Lord. One of the biggest ways he attacks us is through regret. Regret gets to us mentally and if we allow it to it will become a devastating monster. We have to keep it in check, and we can do this by staying in God's Word and talking to God daily. We need to remember what 1 Peter 5:8 tells us; "Be sober-minded; be watchful. Your adversary, the devil, prowls around like a roaring lion, seeking someone to devour."

I hope that all of us are contented when we leave this earth. For me if I never go snow skiing so be it. I have had a wonderful life. For the ones that have unsolved problems with family or friends, go today and resolve it. For those that have unconfessed sins go to your knees and ask forgiveness from God. For those that are ashamed of things you did in your past, let it go, and remember that today is the first day of the rest of your life.

Prayer: Thank you Lord for the joy and contentment that you have allowed me to have in my life. I give you all the praise and glory for all that I have had the pleasure of doing and seeing. Amen.

(Suggested daily Bible readings: Sunday – 1 John 1:8-10; Monday – Psalm 34:4-7; Tuesday – Philippians 3:12-14; Wednesday – Proverbs 15:12-17; Thursday – 2 Timothy 4:6-8; Friday – Isaiah 43:18-19; Saturday – 2 Peter 2:4-11.) A443-17

The hurrier I go the behinder I get

Are you familiar with the old saying, "the hurrier I go, the behinder I get." It came from Lewis Carroll the author of children's book Alice's Adventures in Wonderland and Through the Looking-Glass. These are well known favorites of children and adults alike and have been around since the 1800's.

There are many people just as I am, and this statement fits all of us well. Most of us tend to take on more responsibility than we should and when deadlines approach for these jobs to be done we get in a hurry up mode and frantically start worrying about what we are going to do.

For me I have found that most of my problems come from distractions, and then I drop off into complacency. There are many things I want and need to accomplish; however, I have allowed myself to become involved with other insignificant side items. Once I do this, I become anxious about completing the tasks before me and many times accept the outcome much below what I know I could have done.

As Christians and church members we go about God's work pretty much in the same way. We meet and see people every day that we should be sharing the good news about Jesus with and we pass them by saying, "I'll talk to them later." As with our projects at home and work, our Christian witnessing becomes something we put off until we are pushed into a corner about talking to people. Then we feel the anxiety and frustration because of our own inept attitudes. Witnessing becomes a chore instead of a joy we get when we share the gospel. People are receptive but because we feel unworthy or unmotivated, our friends and family suffer by not having someone speak to them about their eternal salvation.

All of us put things off until tomorrow that need to be done today. During my lifetime I have seen very few people that are so organized that all their day follows a patterned routine. Even these non-procrastinators slip occasionally and fall behind.

We need to realize that each day we need to talk with the Lord and ask Him to guide us and direct in the way He wants us to go. If we will do this then our days will be much happier, and more fruit will come from our labor. We are told in Matthew 5:14, "You are the light of the world…"

With this being said we need to go forth and do the Lord's work and it doesn't matter where we are or what we are doing. We should also complete our earthly task on time and not allow distractions to take away our goals. Should we do this I firmly believe we would become more organized and less complacent.

Prayer: O Lord guide me in all that I do. Lead me in the paths that you have laid out for me and keep me from worldly objections. Amen.

(Suggested daily Bible readings: Sunday – Proverbs 10:19-23; Monday – Psalm 40:6-10; Tuesday – Acts 4:31; Wednesday – John 4:4-26; Thursday – Isaiah 63:7-14; Friday – Daniel 12:1-4; Saturday – Jude 1:16-25.) A177-12

Be an extraordinary person

Ex-NFL Coach Jimmy Johnson use to tell his players, "The difference between ordinary and extraordinary is that little extra." What a tremendous truth in this one little statement and it must have worked for Coach Johnson because he was a highly successful football coach.

I have used this phrase in many of the talks I have given whether it was speaking at a Chamber of Commerce banquet or giving a devotional to a church group. This is one statement that can be used in anything. It has been used repeatedly in the workplace trying to encourage employees to give more than is expected of them. I have noticed that when you expect more from someone and give them the tools to work with, they will exceed your expectations.

It amazes me why people find it hard to give more time to God's work. Many have told me that the church will work you to death if you let it, and a lot of this is true. What about the time not spent with church work but during your everyday vocation? Are you doing anything extra to tell people about the saving grace of Jesus Christ?

Is your livelihood worth looking at? Do people see you going above and beyond expectations of your work and family life?

Many of us talk a good game; however, we all fall into the category of, "After all is said and done, more is said than done." We need to move past this and commit to what we are doing and give that little "extra" we are speaking of. If only a few of us would move forward with our commitments and complete them this world would be a better place.

We read about Jesus' calling of Simon, Andrew, James, and John in the gospel of Mark chapter 1:16-20. These men immediately dropped what they were doing and followed Jesus without question. Each one of them was willing to go the extra mile to be a disciple of Jesus. How many of us today will do this?

It is my prayer that we will turn from our ordinary Christian attitudes to extraordinary disciple attitudes. Will you be the first one to do this?

Prayer: O Lord I praise you for every day you give me on this earth. I pray that I will be a disciple for you and get myself out of the way. Amen.

(Suggested daily Bible readings: Sunday – 1 Samuel 2:18-21; Monday – Luke 9:23-27; Tuesday – 1 Kings 20: 1-22; Wednesday – Mark 1:16-20; Thursday – Psalm 4:1-3; Friday – 2 Timothy 1:8-12; Saturday – Ezekiel 22:30.) A180-12

Distractions that hinder God's call

When we accept Christ as our Lord and Savior, we accept His call to go forth from our sinful nature and do His will. There are so many of us that try and hold on to our sinful ways after giving our heart to Jesus that we miss the blessings that He has for us.

I had a close friend that I worked with for many years who accepted Christ as a young man but would not give up his worldly ways. He, as many young boys and girls in their late teens, hung out with his so-called friends and pursued the ways of drinking alcohol and doing things unbecoming of a Christian. I did not meet this friend until he, as one might say, sowed his wild oats. During his time of drinking he married a girl that was pregnant because it was the right thing to do. He wasn't sure if it was his baby but he took on the responsibility of being a husband and a father. These were back in the days before paternity tests and the word of the mother was taken as the truth.

I met this man at church because he had gotten his life straight and wanted to raise his child in a Christian home and environment. He knew what God wanted him to be and do and once again got in the

Word of God and became a tremendous worker in the church and a God-fearing witness in the workplace and community. God had tremendous plans for this man and he was answering God's call but outside influences kept hitting at him because of his belief and Christian stand he had for Jesus.

He reminded me of Nehemiah when God called him to rebuild the wall around Jerusalem. Nehemiah answered God's call and the Lord furnished everything that he would need to rebuild the wall. He had outside influences that would try and get him off of what God had called him to do but Nehemiah kept his faith and would not give into temptation. He had a priest from within his own people that even tried to lure him away from God's plan but Nehemiah again relented.

Nehemiah demonstrated an understanding of God's call over his life. He pursued his goals with commitment and a reliance on God. He provided encouragement, organization, and authority for the reconstruction project.

My friend resisted many outside obstacles that faced him, however it was an inside problem that finally took him down into Satan's grip. His wife gave way to the call of other men and it tore this family apart. When this happened my friend lost his way and got out of church. He eventually remarried but never came back to the ministry of Christian witnessing and living that he once knew. He has now gone home to be with the Lord and I miss my friend and the many long talks he and I used to have. Even though he lost his desire to be a witness, he knew the Lord and I know that he is in heaven now. I often wonder how many blessings he missed out on when he quit working for the Lord here on earth and gave in to the world again.

Prayer: Lord God, thank you for the opportunity of knowing this friend and the many good times we had on earth. I pray that he is singing praises to you at this time and that you will bless those he left behind. Amen.

(Suggested daily Bible readings: Sunday – 1 Peter 4:12-19; Monday – Nehemiah 6:1-19; Tuesday – Hebrews 12:3-11; Wednesday – Leviticus 26:9-20; Thursday – Philippians 1:3-11; Friday – Amos 5:16-20; Saturday – Romans 8:19-30.) A314-15

Time waits on no one

I am sure that many people are just like me and sit down occasionally and wonder where time has gone. It seems like only yesterday that I was beginning my career in the newspaper business and that has been over 40 years ago. It wasn't so long ago that my wife and I were newlyweds. I vividly remember the days of when my children were born and the days of their youth and activities. Now that I am a senior adult and retired from all the activities that I once had, I realize that life waits on no one.

Many of us, when we were adolescents, couldn't wait until we were teenagers, then we couldn't wait to be 21 so we would be legal for many things. We couldn't wait until we moved out of our parents' house and could get a place of our own. Having the opportunity to become an adult and make decisions for ourselves was a situation we wanted to have.

As we became busy with earning a living, finding the right person to marry, having children, and raising a family, time was passing us by. For the most of us, our future depended on what the Lord had in store for us and we looked to Him for guidance. We were busy planning for the future and now that we have reached our golden years on earth we are looking to that day when the Lord calls us home wondering where has all the years gone?

James tells us in 4:14 "…that life is a vapor that appears for a little time and then vanishes away". For those of us that have seen our children raised and our grandchildren are wishing for the same things we wished for when we were young, we realize life is only a fleeting moment.

My wife, children, and grandchildren are true blessings that I could have never imagined having when I was a young person seeking the world. Having my eyes fixed on the Living God has given me the strength and fortitude to fight off evil desires and stay focused on where the Lord wanted me to be. Yes, I see many in the world today that have all of the fantasies of the world but can they say that they have been truly happy at where life has taken them in the past.

As young people we all looked to the future of where we wanted to go and what we wanted to be, however for those of us that are Christian know that our future is in the hands of the Lord and we should strive to be in His will each and every day. For those of us that have reached our golden years often think about the past and how fast it has gone by, however it has all been worth it because we know where our future will be.

Prayer: Thank you Lord for your love and promise of eternal life. Thank you for the time you have given me on this earth and for the family, friends, and co-workers that you have allowed me to have. Amen.

(Suggested daily Bible readings: Sunday – John 7:1-8; Monday – Genesis 29:15-30; Tuesday – Hebrews 1:8-12; Wednesday – Deuteronomy 28:58-67; Thursday – James 4:13-17; Friday – Psalm 31:14-18; Saturday – Revelation 22:12-17.) A317-15

God's love is unending

Sitting here in the Georgia mountains on a crisp, beautiful morning, I am very aware of how God takes care of His earth and the creatures He put on it.

My wife and I are enjoying the fruits of our motorhome along with some of our grandchildren and their parents. The Lord refreshed this forest during the night with a rain that lasted for a while.

Sleeping inside the motorhome while the rain was coming down was a little piece of Heaven in itself. No one moved around during the night because all of us have the peace and satisfaction that only the Lord can provide.

As the morning light shined through our windows I got up and went outside for some alone time with the Lord. As I talked with Him, I could see the beauty of His creation and was most thankful for what He was showing me.

It seemed that the leaves on the trees were very perky due to the moisture they had received. The lake was calm and peaceful and was waiting on its visitors for the day.

I can only believe that each one of us during our days on earth can be revived each day through our relationship with the Lord. When we accept Jesus as our Lord and Savior and turn our life over to Him what fear should we have of what may come at us during our time on earth.

God's unending love for us and His consistent mercy on us should be all the inspiration we would ever need. Knowing that our final home is eternity with God and the gentleness and peace that only He can provide, should be what we look for and desire each and every day of our life.

In 1 John 4:16 we are told, "And we have known and believed the love that God has for us. God is love, and he who abides in love abides in God and God in him."

As my family and I are enjoying the beauty of God's earth and loving the good times that He is allowing us to have we all realize that this is a great time on earth, however heaven is going to be so much better. God loves all of us in a way that we cannot imagine and gives us hope that we will be with Him in eternity.

Enjoy the beauty of the earth but realize it is only temporary. Realize that the way God cares for His earth is small compared to how much He loves us.

Prayer: What a beautiful temporary home you have given us Lord. Thank you for showing how magnificent you are through the beauty of the earth and the way you take care of all your creatures on it. Thank you for loving me and the promise of being with you in eternity. Amen.

(Suggested daily Bible readings: Sunday – Genesis 2:8-17; Monday – James 1:2-8; Tuesday – Hosea 14:5-7; Wednesday – 1 Peter 3:1-7; Thursday – Psalm 19:1-6; Friday – Matthew 6:28-34; Saturday – Ecclesiastes 3:1-15.) A284-14

Having the courage to do what is right

In today's age many of us are met with situations that could or could not be the right thing to do. We must make a quick decision and whatever decision we make could affect the livelihood for others. Some of the time looking at the world's desires leads us into an uncomfortable place knowing that what we do is wrong, yet we don't want to displease any of our peers, depending on where we are at this certain time.

Knowing the truth and telling the truth is something you don't have to remember. Standing on God's promises and listening to His voice is something we don't have to remember because we have the courage to take a stand and it is the correct one. God will never lead us astray even though the world is telling us something different.

Every day of our lives we have opportunities to display our love for the Lord through our actions and words. What we say can affect us in a positive or a negative way. One of the verses in the Bible that we need to memorize and say to ourselves daily is: Psalm 27:1, "The Lord is my light and my salvation; Whom shall I fear? The Lord is the strength of my life; Of whom shall I be afraid?"

As we walk our daily path this verse should be first and foremost on our minds. Even the most perilous and ardent tasks that we face will be more simple and easier for us to accomplish.

Society in today's world can be very cruel. We see some of our family, friends, coworkers, or others being mistreated because they do not have the stamina to stand up for themselves or they do not know the Lord personally and have their faith and trust in Him. How many times have you seen someone be the brunt end of a joke or idle talk when you know this is not true? Have you ever taken a stand and spoken in favor of this person when you are in the minority however you knew that what was being said was incorrect or wrong?

Our movies and television shows of today and the past generation have given us false images of what is good and how we can mistreat others. Now, don't get me wrong, there have been some terrific shows and movies as well; however, our earthly desires and nature want to see violence and then put into our minds that this is real and we can act this way in the real world. During my career in the newspaper industry I have witnessed and seen firsthand that people don't want to read the good news. They want to hear and read about what is happening to people around them and want to know the troubles others are having. This is what we are teaching our future generations. Again, please don't misinterpret what I am saying. We do need to know the news of today and what is going on around us, but we also need to know the good news and try to be a part of it. Bad news can always have a positive spin to it, but we should never weaken the severity of it.

The next time you see or hear about your family member or neighbor being belittled, whether they are in the right or wrong, stand up for them because they are human and one of God's children. When someone is down and out it is a good time for witnessing to them because they are trying to find their way back to the truth and the light. Will you have the courage to take a stand and be a part of the solution instead of contributing to the problem?

Prayer: Father God, thank you for the opportunities that you give me to share my faith with others. I pray that I will never lead someone astray or misspeak about them. Guide me in a way that will glorify you. Amen.

(Suggested daily Bible readings: Sunday – Psalm 37:25-31; Monday – Philippians 4:10-13; Tuesday – Isaiah 54:4-8; Wednesday – Matthew 10:28; Thursday – 2 Kings 6:16; Friday – 2 Corinthians 4:7-12; Saturday – Proverbs 24:10-12.) A286-14

What will anxiety or worry ever accomplish for us?

Why is it that we are fearful about many things that leads us to worry and have anxiety? People will tell you they do not fear anything, nor do they worry about anything, however I find that hard to believe.

Over my years I have met many people and I don't know if I have ever met anyone that was so stable that nothing ever bothered them. I have met people in high positions of government and business and most of them would tell me about situations that bothered them. I have known many well-versed Christians, some non-Christians, and even some atheist. None of them would ever tell me that all is well, and everything was lovely and peaceful in their lives.

I will tell you that the most contented people I have ever met were Christians and walked the walk as well as talked the talk. Their relationship with God was unbelievable and their outlook on life was positive, even though it wasn't uneventful. Everyone faces trials and tribulations and most everyone has some skeletons in their closet.

My mother-in-law was one of the most God-fearing ladies I ever knew. She read her Bible, attended church as long as possible, loved her family, a great wife to her husband, visited her neighbors and friends, and was one of the most charming people you would ever want to meet. She was all this, but she was also a worrier. I remember a time when a cat was run over and killed on the road in front of her home and she worried if it died hungry. I remember when her son told her he crossed railroad tracks going to teach school, she would call him every morning to tell him to watch for trains. She took worrying to the highest level and at one time it caused her to go into depression.

When this happened, it created a time of worry about her and a void in the family unit. It was a tough time for all the family. With the proper help and counseling she came out of her depression and once again retained her role as a great spiritual leader.

Even the strongest people have their time of despair and doubt. No one is above this and if we are not rooted in the strength of God's love, it is almost impossible to overcome. My favorite verse in the Bible is Philippians 4:13, "I can do all things through Christ who strengthens me." I say this verse repeatedly and rely on it when I am going through a trial, frustration, or any type circumstance.

Worrying can be worse on a person than suffering through a sickness. In my opinion, worrying is a sickness but must be overcome by trusting in the Lord and depending on Him to get you through anything and everything. Since worrying should not be a part of a believer's life, how does one overcome worry? In 1 Peter 5:7, we are instructed to "cast all your anxiety on him because he cares for you." God does not want us to carry around the weight of problems and burdens. In this verse, God is telling us to give Him all our worries and concerns. Why does God want to take on our problems? The Bible says it is because He cares for us. God is concerned about everything that happens to us. No worry is too big or too small for His attention. When we give God our problems, we are told in the book of Philippians He promises to give us the peace which transcends all understanding.

Prayer: Thank you Lord for taking all my worry, fear, and anxiety and giving me peace and understanding. Amen.

(Suggested daily Bible readings: Sunday – Philippians 4:6-7; Monday – Psalm 55:22-23; Tuesday – 1 Peter 5:6-7; Wednesday – Proverbs 12:25; Thursday – Luke 12:22-26; Friday – Isaiah 43:1-3; Saturday – Hebrews 13:5-11.) A306-14

It's not what you say; it's how you say it!

I saw a short video the other day that made a tremendous impact on me. It showed a man sitting on a sidewalk asking for donations. The man had a sign next to him that read "I am blind, please help."

Many people were walking by but only a few were dropping money into the can he had. People were reading the sign however they weren't thinking about his handicap and the problems he was experiencing.

It's this way every day for most of us. We see people in need and don't stop to think about their needs because we are so busy trying to satisfy our desires. We are so preoccupied with what we are doing or where we are going that we don't notice the ones around us, especially the ones that can use our help. Life is passing us by, and we don't even realize the joy we are missing by helping our brothers and sisters in need.

All of us need to realize that at any time we can go from having what we need such as a job, food on the table, a roof over our head, and a family we can depend on to nothing at all. The ones of us that have what we need should realize that not everyone around us are as well off as we are. Many people do not want others to know they are hurting but will give signs of need that we should be able to see and read.

I know firsthand about having too much pride when I was in a time of need but thanks to Godly people around me, they saw through my piety and offered much needed help. Then there are those who actually ask for help and we should hear their plea and be there for them.

Jesus was the greatest example when He came to deal with people. He met their needs and gave Himself to die for all of our sins so that we may have eternal salvation. What more could anyone ever ask for. Jesus never missed a chance to help anyone and offers eternity to anyone that believes and has faith in Him.

All of us need to read other people's needs and see how we can help, just as Jesus did. The blind man who was sitting on the street could hear the people passing in front of him however his sign was not attracting the attention he needed. One lady came by, stopped in front of him, picked up his sign turned it over and wrote new words. Her new sign read, "It's a beautiful day and I can't see it."

Her words attracted many more people because it was not stating what was wrong with him, simply stating that he could not enjoy what everyone around him was seeing. A lot more people understood his need because they could visualize what he didn't have and gave generously to him. All of us need to pay more attention to those around us and help them in their time of need, especially those that need Jesus. All of us need to be extremely generous when it comes to our Christian witness.

Prayer: Lord I pray that I can be like you and see the needs of those around me. Thank you for the ones that have helped me in the past. Thank you for your saving grace. Amen.

(Suggested daily Bible readings: Sunday – Acts 2:44-47; Monday – Ecclesiastes 5:8-9; Tuesday – Romans 12:9-13; Wednesday – Leviticus 23:22; Thursday – Philippians 1:1-11; Friday – Psalm41:1; Saturday – Galatians 3:5-9.) A310-14

Love is patient, love is kind

During the holiday seasons I watched a lot of Hallmark channel movies. Most of these movies are oriented to the season and most of them are geared toward showing love for someone or for showing love toward one another. These are great movies that always have great purpose to them, do not show immorality, no vulgar scenes, and do not use any profanity. They are genuinely good family movies.

These movies show a lot of people being brought together through circumstances other than what we expect in everyday life. Actually, it could be everyday life, we just choose not to recognize it because it may get in way of our earthly desires or wants, and we fail to recognize what is right in front of our nose.

Many of you may have seen the Christmas in Conway movie. It was about a man wanting to give his dying wife a final wish and give her a ride on a ferris wheel until she passed away. The only thing he could do was to purchase one and put it in his backyard which was in a historic district of town. His next-door neighbor, which had grievances that went back to both families' grandfathers, was trying to be the Christmas showplace of the town and complained about what was going on next door with the ferris wheel.

The man, a staunch, self-righteous man, had trouble getting along with people and most of the problem was his grief that he was carrying inside because of his sick wife. He had trouble working with the hospice nurse who came to live with them until his wife would eventually go home to be with the Lord. The man had hope he could take care of his wife without the help of trained professionals.

He had trouble with a young man that eventually helped him construct his project because the young man had stolen something from him in the past. He had no faith in the young man. Yet the young man turned his life around because the man's dying wife was a former schoolteacher of his and forgave him of his problems and showed him how he could turn his life around.

We are told in 1 Corinthians 13:4-7; "Love is patient, love is kind. It does note envy, it does not boast. It is not rude, it is not self-seeking, it is not easily angered, it keeps no record of wrongs. Love does not delight in evil but rejoices with the truth. It always protects, always trusts, always hopes, always perseveres." Verse 8 also starts, "Love never fails."

As the story ends the man learned from the hospice nurse that not only did, she cares for his wife, she cared for him by not letting him run her off and helped him overcome some of the grief that he was harboring. The young man didn't give up on the man either and showed him that all he wanted was forgiveness because he wasn't the same person he was in the past. He had actually done something with his life and just wanted to be a help to others, especially the dying lady because of her faith in him and her nurturing him in the right direction. Both show unconditional love for the man.

The lady next door, that wanted all the glory for her Christmas showplace, eventually came around because she witnessed the love the man gave to his wife in erecting a ferris wheel in his backyard overcoming the obstacles he faced from her, the law, and others.

It is my hope that all of us as we face each day of the rest of our lives, is that we will look around and help those in need. Many are going to say they don't want our help, but we can help them through love and prayerful concern. Each one of us will need to exercise our faith, hope, and love in our neighbors and friends.

1 Corinthians 13:13 tells us; "And now these three remain, faith, hope and love. But the greatest of these is love."

Prayer: Lord I pray that I will be the shining example that you expect me to be and that I can love everyone, even the unlovable. Amen.(Suggested daily Bible readings: Sunday – 1 John 2:3-6; Monday – Deuteronomy 1:26-33; Tuesday – 1 Peter 4:7-11; Wednesday – Malachi 1:2-5; Thursday – John 21:15-19; Friday – Song of Solomon 8:7; Saturday – Revelation 3:19-22.)A312-14

Why do we treat our love ones worse than others?

Something that I have noticed about many husbands, wives, brothers, sisters, or other family members is that when it comes to making decisions or wanting something done most of us tend to treat our loved ones and the ones closest too us worse than we do others.

When I retired, I felt making major decisions concerning small or major problems would come to an end. When in the newspaper business the buck stopped at my desk and all the employees relied on my decisions to be the correct ones. If I didn't have a ready answer, then I was expected to find the right one by going to the right people. I wasn't used to people questioning my decision and they took my final answer as the truth.

Now that I am retired from the newspaper industry and continue working part-time from home alongside of my wife, I find myself in a different type of environment and new rules to abide by. Even though we have been married for over 40 years and I know her and love her more than anyone else on earth, I sometimes find myself asking or telling her what to do about certain situations and she questions me about my decisions. I guess I have the same type expectations of her as I did with the employees I worked with. Then, again on the other hand, she retired from teaching school after 21 years of working with special needs children. We had two totally different careers, different type managerial experience, yet similar in nature. We both worked with the public.

I find myself thinking that she should understand what I want and what I am talking about when we are working together and expect her to act accordingly. On the other hand, she does the same with me when she speaks to me, with the exception that sometimes she wants to talk down to me as she has so many years for children to understand her.

I wonder if this is typical in all families. I have witnessed on so many occasions a young husband belittling his wife for something she had no idea of what to do and he had not taken the time to explain to her all the facts. It was his way and she should understand that his hollering and badgering her was just going to be a way of life. Then again, I have seen other couples that wouldn't speak to each other for days because one of them expected their spouse to read their mind and do what they had no idea to do. It seems that the more we love someone the more we expect them to understand they need to do what we want before we tell them. Billy Graham once wrote that there are three elements to a successful marriage: Love, maturity, and faith. Marriage must be Christ centered for the marriage and home to be successful. In today's mindset of the world, too many young people enter a marriage without any of the three essential elements mentioned by Mr. Graham and expect to have a fruitful relationship and family.

In Galatians 5:22-23 we are told, "But the fruit of the Spirit is love, joy, peace, forbearance, kindness, goodness, faithfulness, gentleness and self-control. Against such things there is no law."

I love my wife with all of my heart and soul, yet I find myself treating her on occasions worse than I would anyone else. Why is this? In no way would I ever do anything to hurt her yet sometimes I say things or give facial expressions that seem mean spirited.

There are many people in this world today that don't have what we have and that is a Christ led marriage and family. Even though there are misunderstandings and difference of opinions, we know in the end we love each other, and no one can take that away. Spouses and family members are easy targets for us to take out our frustrations. It shouldn't be this way!

Prayer: Thank you Lord for my wife and her love. You have blessed us so much and for this I give you all the praise and glory. Give me wisdom and strength to treat her as you would have me to do. Amen.(Suggested daily Bible readings: Sunday – Philippians 4:4-7; Monday – Psalm 34:17-20; Tuesday - Luke 10:27; Wednesday – Malachi 2:13-15; Thursday – 2 Timothy 3:10-17; Friday – Genesis 4:1-26; Saturday – 2 Peter 3:8-13.)A246-13

You are never too old to learn

As I get older the more I want to know. The carefree life of my younger years is past me and learning new and exciting things is something I want to do.

My wife and I decided that we would not become involved in the Facebook movement. We were too old to be involved with this type social media and felt it could be a harmful adventure for us or someone else. Eventually our children talked us into becoming readers of Facebook especially after we found out they were posting photos of us and our grandchildren. Now I was curious and wanted to be in the loop of what was being posted and what was being said.

Both of us are now on Facebook and still believe it can be a hurtful avenue for some. However, I have found many friends from the past and renewed many acquaintances of yesteryear. I have also found many great spiritual avenues and a great number of wise sayings and quotes.

One of the quotes I read was, "No matter how good or bad you think life is, wake up each day and be thankful for life. Someone somewhere else is fighting to survive."

Not many of us really think about our present situation being a good one especially if we are not feeling our best. We are thinking "oh woe is me" without consideration of whom in the world, our state, our community, or maybe our own family is worse off than we are. Don't get me wrong, for some of us really have some problems and it seems the only way for us to be relieved of them is for God to step in and help us.

If we trust in the Lord to help us, we must be open to the various ways this could happen. Many times, we are looking so hard for heaven's door to open that we miss the window God has propped open for us. So many of us are pessimist and we miss so many blessings. We need to remember what Harry Truman once said, "A pessimist is one who makes difficulties of his opportunities and an optimist is one who makes opportunities of his difficulties."

Sometimes we get focused on one way to do things and that is our way. We are looking so hard for God to answer us the way we want to be answered instead of looking around and visualizing what God is really saying to us. We become stubborn and lose faith because of our own shortcomings and loss of reality. God will always supply an answer we just need to be willing to accept what He sends us or tells us.

As we grow older and, hopefully, wiser, I believe we understand that God has gotten us to where we are despite our misunderstandings as a human being. I am more prone to look and listen to what God is telling me because I really understand that my time on earth is limited and I know that I am going to be with Him soon. God really does give wisdom to those who wait on Him and studies His Word.

Prayer: Thank you again Lord for the time on earth you have given me. I praise you in everything and ask that I seek you in all that I do. Amen.

(Suggested daily Bible readings: Sunday – Leviticus 19:32; Monday –Luke 2:49-52; Tuesday – Psalm 71:14-21; Wednesday – Colossians 1:9-14; Thursday –Ecclesiastes 12:1-8; Friday –Philippians 1:3-6; Saturday – Proverbs 20:29.)A244-13

CPSIA information can be obtained
at www.ICGtesting.com
Printed in the USA
BVHW061411271221
624935BV00011B/397